SWIM BETTER

SWIM BETTER

A Guide to Greater Efficiency for Swimmers and Instructors

Bob Colyer, P.E.D.

CSCAA Master Coach

Sun on Earth™ Books
Heathsville, Virginia

Published by Sun on Earth™ Books

www.sunonearth.com

Illustrations by Laura Bushinski — laurabushinski.carbonmade.com

Publisher's Cataloging-in-Publication Data
Colyer, Robert.
   Swim better / Robert Colyer.— lst ed.
      p. cm.
   ISBN: 978-1-883378-68-4
         1. Swimming—Instruction.
         I. Title.

GV837.7 S95 2014
797.2'1—dc22

Library of Congress Control Number: 2014956682

For Doc & Marge and, always & all ways, Allyn

What we hope ever to do with ease, we must learn first to do with diligence.

— Samuel Johnson (1709-1784)

Contents

Better Swimming

An Acquired Skill

Swimming is an unnatural act. Humans are not born with a natural capacity to adjust to continuous immersion in water. Reflexive crawling actions may help an infant learn to "swim," but for children and adults, swimming is a complex skill that becomes increasingly more difficult to learn as one grows older. Rarely is a self-taught swimmer efficient. Almost all good swimmers are the products of good instruction by good instructors.

What is good swimming instruction?

It is one that guides swimmers through a process where weak (less efficient) swimming skills are **un**learned and then **re**learned to improve the efficiency of aquatic locomotion. That's it.

Presented here are two underlying **Fundamentals** of better swimming, plus two **Rules** to utilize, followed by applications to specific strokes—a simple, common pathway of progressive skills that help build swimmers' and instructors' understanding and confidence.

While competitive swimmers and coaches can benefit, the primary goal of this book is to assist instructors and self-instructed swimmers to develop highly-efficient skills for swimming faster, farther, with less exertion, and a great deal of enjoyment.

Two Fundamentals for Swimming Efficiency

FUNDAMENTAL

Efficient stroking can be achieved in two ways—by decreasing resistance and/or by increasing propulsion

The first step toward greater efficiency is producing as long and as sleek a swimmer's body position in the water as possible. Once that has been accomplished, the swimmer can focus on applying propulsive force.

FUNDAMENTAL

Stroking is moving the body past the hand rather than the hand past the body

The efficient swimmer is able to optimize the distance the body travels per stroke, thus decreasing the number of strokes needed per pool length.

Two Rules for Swimming Efficiency

RULE 1

Make it Different

Unlearning and learning again is what distinguishes the method of teaching adult swimmers. The new movement and behavior must be as unrelated as possible to the old, or at least perceived that way.

RULE 2

Develop Quality over Quantity

Do only what is efficient, and then stop. There is little to be gained—and a lot to be lost—by swimming laps with a less-than-efficient stroke.

Getting Started

Push-Off & Glide—The Basis for Everything

Being on the side (which follows Rule 1) makes the swimmer more

fish-like and is the key to efficient swimming.

1 Begin at the pool wall

Hold the wall lightly with one hand (let's say the right) on the gutter

or pool's edge, feet together on the wall a foot or two below the surface and pointing toward the side (not the pool bottom), knees

bent, with left arm and hand stretched out toward the opposite

wall.

2 First movement: release and lift the arm

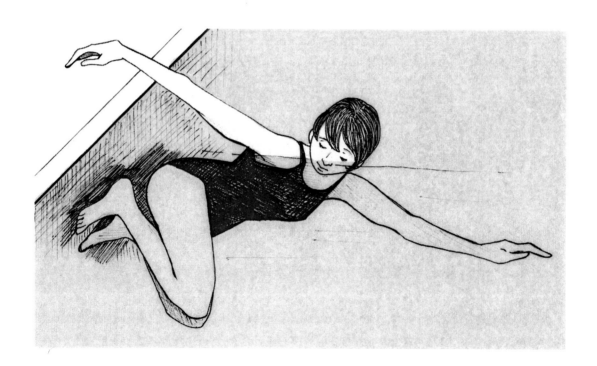

Just release and lift, and let the body sink. It's a simple action—no need to reach or extend the legs. Just **lift** the arm, **relax**, and **sink**, keeping the feet in contact with the wall. This needs to be repeated only once or twice because it will be done continually as strokes are developed.

3 **READY - lift and, while sinking, extend the right arm to meet the left—hand over hand**

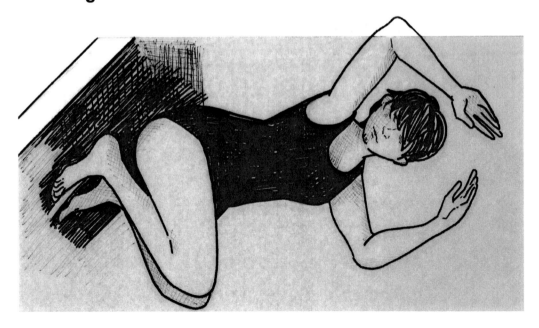

Just pause and relax (the key to everything) during and after this simple action. Gradually, done just a few times, this overall movement of lifting, sinking, and extending hand over hand ("ears between the elbows"), while **maintaining the feet on the wall**, becomes a single, blended, smooth and efficient action to begin the progression.

4 **GO - Extend the legs and push off under water, with the body stretched as long as possible on its side to produce a long glide.**

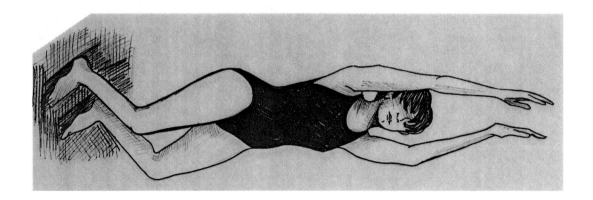

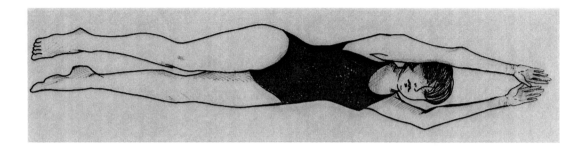

This will need to be repeated so that glides can get farther and farther from the wall. Experiment and adjust the depth of the feet on the wall and/or the angle of the bent knees (90° is optimal) to get more push for gliding distance. Swimmers who maintain one hand on top of the other can optimize their narrow profile.

Efficient swimming starts off with the realization that every stroke includes the glide phase described above. Elementary Backstroke, Sidestroke, and Breaststroke were created as gliding strokes. Front and Back Crawl are really alternating glides on left and right sides through the front and back. And even Butterfly uses a glide when swum most efficiently.

5 Repeat these steps on the other side, holding on to the wall or gutter with the left hand

Repeating the process on this other side should take less time, but be sure to have the discipline to do only the action(s) called for in each step of the progression.

Pausing long enough to sink, placing feet on the wall a little higher or lower, pushing through the chest, keeping a dynamic balance, and developing the longest possible glide on both sides are more than enough for a swimmer to work on before adding specific stroke elements.

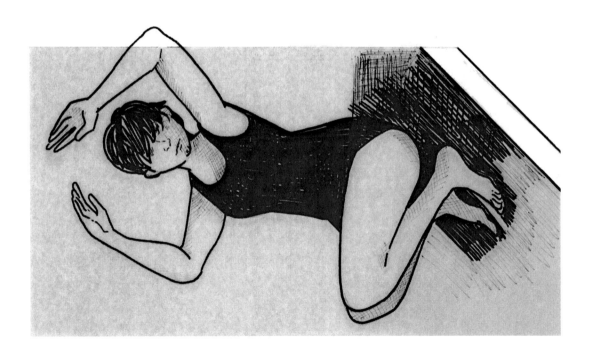

Develop the habit of going through all steps unhurriedly and in a relaxed manner. It's the key to continue throughout the learning process toward better swimming.

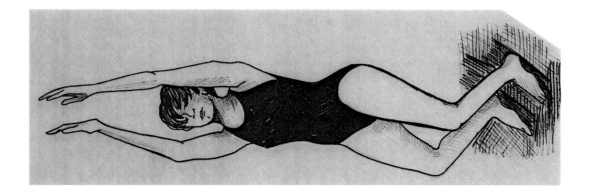

Stroking

Once a dynamic balance for push-off and glide has been developed, the swimmer can begin to add specific stroke elements.

For each stroke, the head should be kept in the water to balance the body around the lower chest (its center of buoyancy), thus keeping the hips near the water's surface to minimize resistance. Don't confuse this with floating. This is a dynamic balance while the body is in motion, which is Step 2 for each stroke.

All swim strokes share more than just the push-off and glide, however. For each, there is a propulsive phase and a recovery phase, as well as a glide of varying length.

All strokes need to maintain pressure against non-moving water by adjusting the hands or feet. This varies with individuals, and it's more a tactile feeling than a specific path to be followed (see Fundamental B).

Each stroke that follows is taught from the push-off and glide, as if the swimmer were learning it for the first time.

Crawl Stroke

Let's face it. This is the stroke that counts, the real basis that swimmers are judged on, regardless of their proficiency in other strokes.

Crawl Stroke is not the same as Freestyle, which is a competitive swimming term for allowing any stroke. Being the fastest stroke, Crawl Stroke is usually swum for Freestyle.

The front Crawl is not swum on the front, but side-to-side **through** the front. It should feel analogous to the relaxed rhythm of long-distance ice-skating or cross-country skiing.

1 **Use the Push-Off & Glide (Page 15) to create momentum**

2 **Establish the glide position for the stroke**

When momentum begins to slow, stroke the top arm close to the body, down to the thigh to establish the glide position for the Crawl Stroke. Practice once or twice on each side.

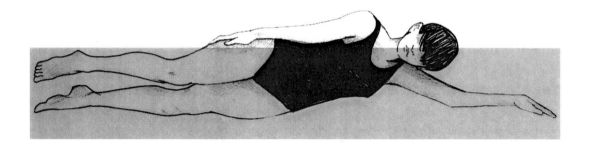

3 Add a narrow flutter kick

Kick from the hips with relaxed ankles—more for maintaining balance than for momentum. Remember that the energy cost of kicking is much greater (about a 5:2 ratio) than for arm strokes.

Be sure to pause and establish the glide before initiating the kick, especially keeping the lead arm angled slightly downward.

The kick should take the swimmer across the pool, or close enough so that the same action can be repeated from and on the other side. Practice on both sides until each side feels comfortable and relaxed.

Stay on the side, not flat in the water. The body position on its side creates less resistance and develops both legs more evenly and effectively.

Do not overkick, either by increasing the rhythm or widening the kick beyond the path made by the torso.

4 Add an arm stroke, beginning with the recovery

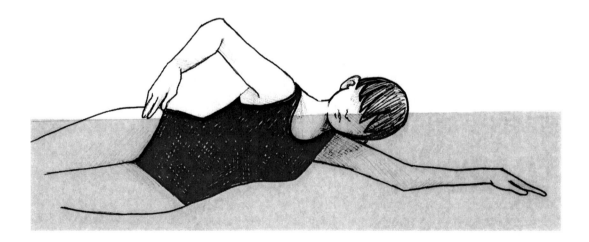

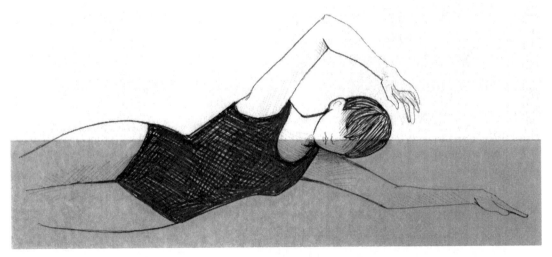

Once the glide position and comfortable kick are established,

begin recovering the top arm from the glide position. The elbow should feel as if lifted on a puppet string, with the lower arm just hanging and the finger tips more or less dragging on the water's surface close to the body, continuing that way until they lead the arm, still relaxed (not overextended), on its downward angle "into a sleeve" for the catch.

5 "Catch" the water with a high elbow

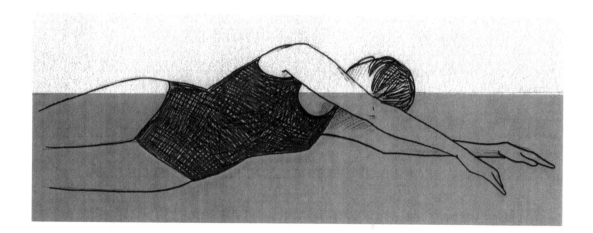

Throughout the recovery and propulsion, the elbow remains higher than the hand. The catch establishes a propulsive position with the hand and forearm anchored (as if over a barrel) to enable the body to move past.

6 Create a surge

From the catch position, body on side, apply leverage against non-moving water to move the body past the stroking hand until the thumb extends to the thigh and pauses in the glide position.

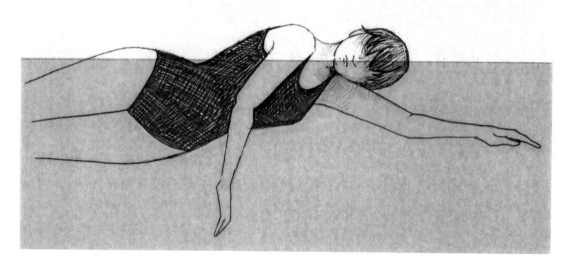

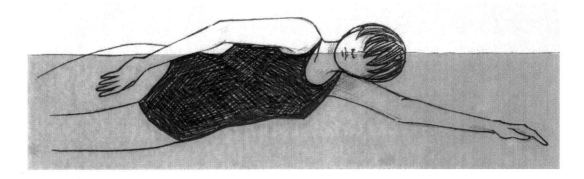

As the body moves past the hand, maintain pressure (inside both upper and lower arm) on the "barrel" by adjusting wrist and open palm.

"Wrap" the hand and forearm around the water until the shoulder passes the hand, and "unwrap" as the stroke is completed down to the thigh.

Obviously, this single, basic arm stroke (Steps 4, 5, and 6) needs to be learned separately on both left and right sides. While doing so, the kick can be minimized or even eliminated.

7 Do no more than this single stroke

Master this single stroke on both the left side and the right, gradually increasing the distance covered by this one complete stroke without adding another. There should be no hurry to do more.

8 Add a second stroke

After optimizing this single stroke (for each side), add a second arm stroke on the same side. Be sure to complete the first stroke to glide position before adding the second as momentum slows.

Again, stick just to two strokes on a single side, gradually increasing the distance covered by using the two surges, and do it separately for each side.

9 Add breathing

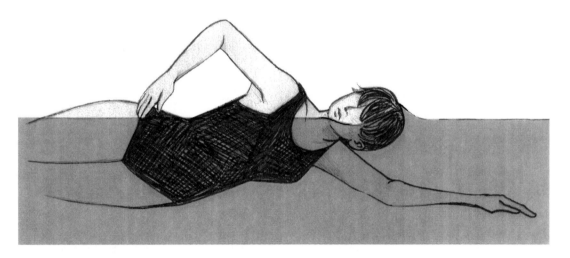

As the top arm recovers during the second stroke, minimal, if any, head rotation is needed. The swimmer inhales ("in your armpit" or "eat your thumb") in the trough of the wave created by the head, which remains at or slightly below water level.

Exhalation, especially through the nose, should be forced, to rid the lungs of as much carbon dioxide as possible. Regardless of the swimmer's preference for breathing side, it is necessary to learn to breathe on each side to learn balance and to proceed to the next step.

10 Add more single-arm strokes

Push off from the end wall for sufficient room to add more single-arm strokes on each side, taking a breath during the recovery phase of each arm stroke.

Swimmers need to work until they can effectively propel themselves for an entire pool length on each of their left and right sides, attempting to do so in the fewest number of strokes possible.

The single-arm drill is impossible to be practiced too much, and it is the drill to be encouraged when swimmers practice on their own.

11 Put both sides together by a series of steps

The key to a learned/relearned crawl stroke is the next step. The swimmer, after the push-off and glide, goes **ten kicks**, and then **switch**es arms (recovering one and stroking with the other) to the gliding position on the other side.

Completing ten comfortable kicks, the swimmer maintains glide position on the downward-angled arm until the recovering hand has passed its shoulder. After this point, as the recovering arm descends into its "sleeve," it transfers momentum to the rigid shoulder girdle, which in turn transfers that momentum to the bottom arm preparing to stroke.

With the bottom arm already angled downward, this enables the bottom hand to catch and initiate the stroke that levers the body past the stroking hand (Fundamental B).

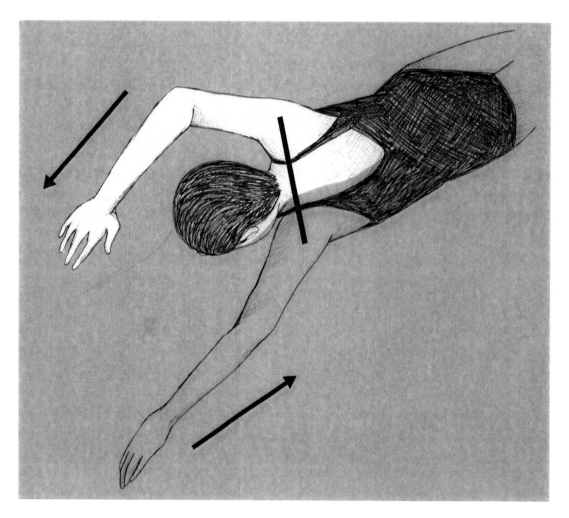

As with the single arm, the swimmer should stroke the bottom arm with a bent elbow, while feeling pressure ("over a barrel") inside both the upper and lower arm as well as the hand.

Once the shoulder of the stroking arm has passed the hand, it transfers momentum, again through the shoulder girdle, as the stroke finishes. This drives the recovering arm to complete the body roll comfortably (not overextended), down into the glide position while the stroking hand finishes at the thigh.

There should be a feeling of riding the glide, as a skater does.

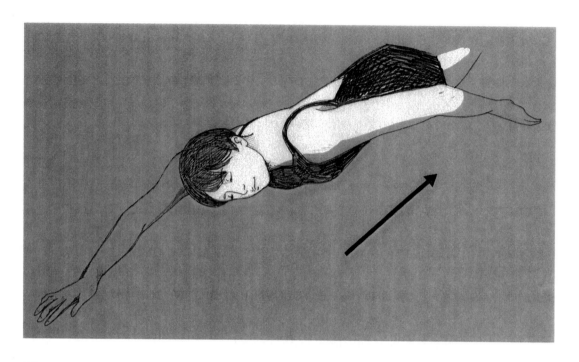

Thus the key to efficient crawl coordination is not to stroke until recovery is near completion. This Crawl timing demands focus and considerable practice, even for accomplished swimmers.

Be content with only occasional success (Rule 2) for a while.

12 Add a second full stroke

Only after the swimmer has mastered ten kicks and a switch (nothing more) separately from each side, will it be time for the next step.

The swimmer is ready to push off and establish glide position, go ten kicks, switch, kick another ten times, and switch again.

The swimmer needs to be limited to just these two switches (one stroke cycle) until they are comfortable and effective.

13 Add breathing

Now the swimmer is ready to add the breathing learned during single-arm stroking, for a full length of ten-kick switching side-to-side. Now is also the time to use the favored side to inhale, but also being sure to **exhale** bubbles (again, forcefully) **to the opposite side** in order to maintain a balanced stroke.

14 Continue to develop the stroke

When comfortable with this forced extension and long strokes, the swimmer can then progress to a six-kick switch. Again, practice until comfortable.

Finally, progress to three kicks. The first of the three kicks is usually a little stronger than the other two (waltz rhythm for the switch) to help the body rotation and the power of the stroking arm on the same side. With practice, this should result in a less mechanical, smooth, relearned Crawl that is indeed different from the swimmer's former struggling stroke.

CRAWL STROKE DRILLS

a. Kick on side (glide position), switching sides after each length, thus always facing same side wall. No need for speed. Stay relaxed for comfortable body balance.

b. Single-arm stroking with kick (easier with other arm in glide position), again switching sides after each pool length (always facing same side wall).

c. Single arm, alternating two strokes using one arm with two using the other, or 3-3.

d. Arm strokes (alternating) alone, preferably without using a pull-buoy® or tube that floats legs but inhibits body roll. This is a good drill for working on the timing introduced in Step 11.

e. Rope drill, described in section for Instructors.

f. Swim with fists, also described for Instructors.

g. Measure progress. Count the number of strokes it takes to swim one length of the pool. This will establish a basis for comparison later on.

Back Crawl Stroke

The Back Crawl is not swum on the back, but side-to-side **through** the back. It has a side-to-side rhythm like ice skating or cross-country skiing for long distances. The Back Crawl is not limited to being a competitive stroke.

1 **Use the Push-Off & Glide (Page 15) to create momentum**

2 **Establish the glide position for the stroke**

When momentum begins to slow, stroke the bottom arm close to the body, down to the thigh. This rotates the body to the opposite side, with shoulders and hips orienting the body toward the back, to establish the glide position. The leading (now the bottom) arm extends at a slightly downward angle, with the shoulder of the top arm above water level. Practice once or twice on each side.

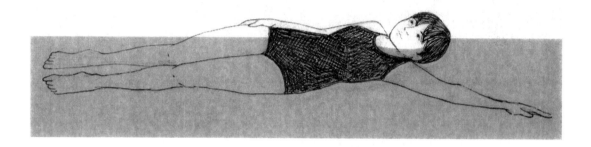

3 Add a narrow flutter kick

Be sure to pause and establish the glide before initiating the kick, especially keeping the lead arm angled slightly downward. Kick from the hips, not the knees—with relaxed ankles—to maintain balance more than for momentum.

The kick should take the swimmer across the pool, or close enough so that the same action can be repeated off the wall on the other side. Practice on both sides until each side feels comfortable and relaxed.

Stay on the side and off the back. This body position creates less resistance and develops both legs more evenly and effectively. Do not overkick, either by rhythm or widening the kick beyond the path made by the torso, keeping it relaxed and narrow.

For an interesting revelation, though, try kicking on the back with just one leg for several kicks, then with just the other. You will be surprised at how much more kick you get from one of your legs than from the other.

4 Add an arm stroke – "Catch" the water with a bent elbow

Once the glide position and a comfortable kick are established, the catch creates a propulsive position with the hand "anchored" against the water as the elbow bends closer to the body. The whole arm "embraces" the water to enable the body to move past.

5 Create a surge

From the catch position, body on side, apply leverage to non-moving water to move the body past the stroking hand/arm until the thumb extends to the thigh and pauses in the glide position.

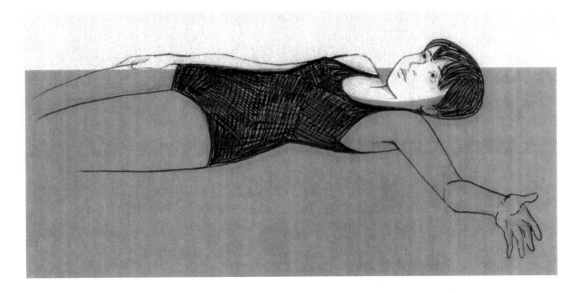

As the body moves past the hand, maintain pressure on the water by adjusting the wrist and open palm.

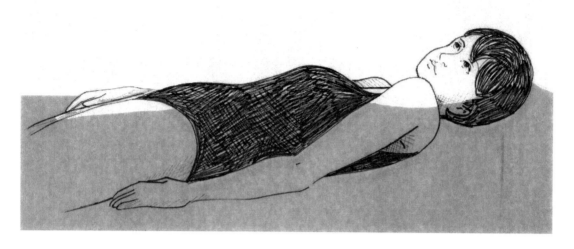

"Wrap" the hand and forearm around the water until the hand reaches shoulder level, and "unwrap" as the stroke is completed down to the thigh.

Obviously, this single, basic arm stroke needs to be learned separately on both left and right sides. While doing so, the kick can be minimized or even eliminated. Finish the stroke with palm down, which elevates the shoulder to facilitate recovery.

6 Recover to the glide position

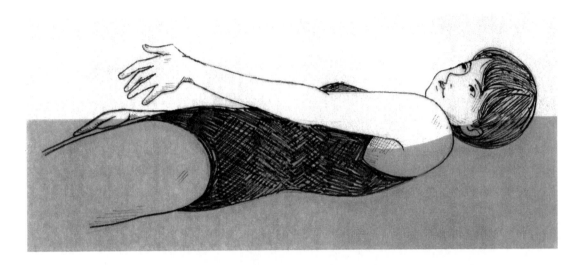

Lift the arm, thumb first, straight up to a vertical position while being rotated so that the little finger is now leading.

Maintain that extension as the arm, relaxed (not overextended),

lowers comfortably (not behind the head) and enters the water to a

slightly downward angle for the glide and the catch.

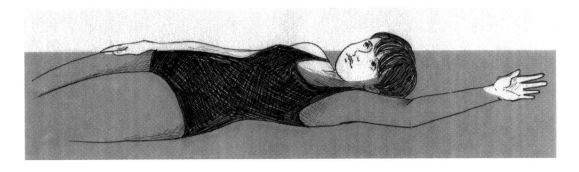

Obviously, this single, basic arm stroke (Steps 4-6) needs to be learned separately on both left and right sides. While doing so, the kick can be minimized or even eliminated.

7 Do no more than this single stroke

Master this single stroke, a relaxed recovery followed by an effective body surge and glide. Do it from a push-off, separately on each side. Gradually increase the distance covered by this one complete stroke without adding another, as per Rule Two. There should be no hurry to do more.

8 Add a second stroke

After optimizing the single stroke (for each side), add a second arm stroke on the same side. Be sure to complete the first stroke to glide position before adding the second, as momentum slows.

Again, stick just to two strokes on a single side, gradually increasing the distance covered by using the two surges, and do it separately for each side.

9 Add breathing

As the top arm recovers during the second stroke, the swimmer inhales. Exhalation occurs during the propulsive phase and should be forced, to rid the lungs of as much carbon dioxide as possible. Do the same on each side to learn balance and to proceed to the next step.

10 Add more single-arm strokes

Push off from the end wall to add more single-arm strokes on each side, taking a breath during the recovery phase of each arm stroke.

Single-arm swimming may be more comfortable and effective beyond two strokes with the non-stroking arm being held at the side. The swimmer will need to work until achieving effective propulsion for an entire pool length on each side, attempting to do so in the fewest number of strokes possible.

11 Put both sides together by a series of steps

The key to a learned/relearned Back Crawl Stroke is the next step. The swimmer, after the push-off and glide, goes **ten kicks**, and then **switch**es arms to the gliding position on the other side. Mastery of this basic move should be the highest priority for student and instructor.

To switch sides, the swimmer starts with the top or recovering arm, lifting it straight up from its glide position on the thigh and keeping it straight.

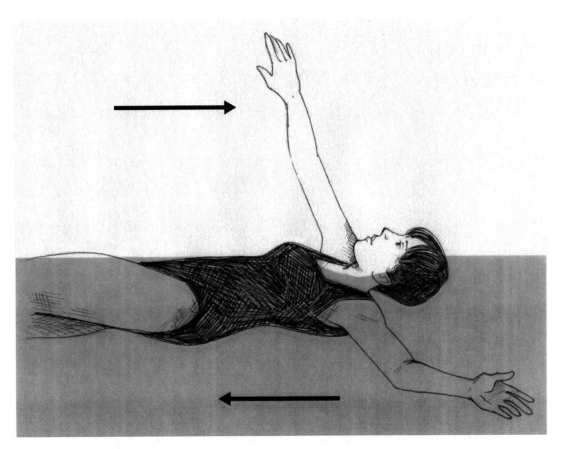

The recovering arm transfers momentum to the shoulder girdle, which in turn transfers momentum to the bottom arm preparing to stroke. The swimmer should stroke the bottom arm with a bent elbow, the whole stroking motion feeling much like a slow-motion throw to optimize the surge of the body.

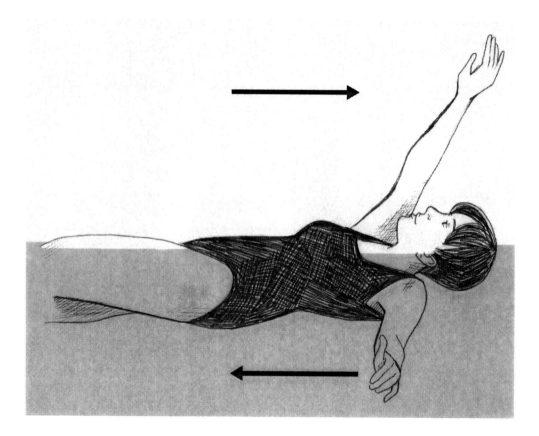

During this stroking motion, the shoulder girdle drives the recovering arm to enter the water pinkie-first, still straight (not overextended), palm down into the glide position while the stroking hand finishes at the thigh.

12 Add a second stroke

After having mastered ten kicks and a switch (nothing more) separately on each side, the swimmer will be ready for the next step—pushing off and establishing the glide position, going ten kicks, switching, kicking another ten times, and switching again.

13 Add Breathing

Adding breathing (forcefully exhaling on one arm and inhaling on the other), the swimmer is limited to just these two strokes until they are comfortable and effective, at which time the swimmer is ready for a full length of ten-kick switching side-to-side.

14 Continue to develop the stroke

When comfortable with this forced extension and long strokes, the swimmer can then progress to a six-kick switch. Again, practice until comfortable.

Finally, progress to three kicks. The first of the three kicks is usually a little stronger than the other two (waltz rhythm for the switch) to help the body rotation and the power of the opposite stroking arm. With practice, this should result in a less mechanical, smooth, relearned Back Crawl Stroke that follows the Fundamentals and Rules.

BACK CRAWL DRILLS

a. Kick on side (glide position), switching sides after each length, thus always facing same side wall.

b. Double arm stroke to feel catch and throwing motion, with or without kicking.

c. Single-arm stroking with kick (easier with non-stroking arm down), again switching sides after each pool length (always facing same side wall). Finish stroke with palm down, to elevate shoulder for easier recovery.

d. Single arm, alternating two strokes using one arm with two using the other, or 3-3.

e. Arm stroke (alternating) alone, preferably without using a pull-buoy® or tube that inhibits body roll.

f. Pole drill, described in section for Instructors.

g. Swim with fists, also described for Instructors.

h. Measure progress. Count the number of strokes it takes to swim one length of the pool. This will establish a basis for comparison later on.

Breaststroke

Breaststroke is the oldest of strokes. It was basically breaststroke that Benjamin Franklin swam in the Delaware River and what Captain Matthew Webb used when he was the first to swim across the English Channel. The stroke to be emphasized here is non-competitive, long, relaxed, and efficient.

1 Use the Push-Off & Glide (Page 15) to create momentum

2 Establish the glide position for the stroke

As momentum begins to slow, rotate to a prone position on the front by dropping the upper shoulder and hip.

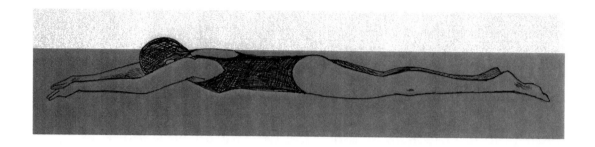

Keep the head and face in the water; and perhaps place one hand on the other to help exaggerate the double-arm, relaxed stretch that is the glide position for the Breaststroke, to which each stroke returns.

Both phases (arms & breath, kick & glide) can be learned from this glide position, in either order.

3 Add arm stroking

As with other strokes, begin with an effective elbows-up catch.

The timing and the basic rounded motion of the upper limbs can begin with a simple rotation of the hands at the wrists, even just rotating the fingers with the thumbs locked.

This smallest movement can then be increased, but with the hands never getting past the chin, just a wide and short ellipse, not long or narrow.

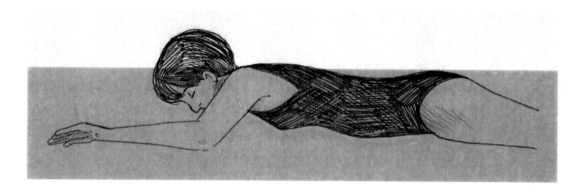

4 Do no more than this single stroke

As with all the strokes, stick to just the push-off, glide, and one propulsive movement of the hands and/or arms. The elbows stay up as they gradually move farther out for the stroke, and are squeezed together for the recovery.

The hands don't need to surface and should be kept below the elbows, arms angled slightly downward for a variety of reasons (less shoulder tension, less tendency to move the hand toward the surface and thus increase resistance, better angle to apply propulsive force from a deep catch).

5 Develop a kick, beginning with the recovery

Obviously, the most difficult task for the Breaststroke is the whip kick, especially for those swimmers who have in the past made a habit of a less than efficient kick on back or front.

Think **heels**. Two aspects are important here. One, recovering the heels first stresses bending at the knees and not at the hips; two, keeping the toes in line with the lower leg (not turned out) on recovery will prevent overstretching knee tendons and ligaments, the source of painful "breaststroker's knee."

6 Prepare to kick by "catching" the water

As the heels reach the butt, then toes can be "unpointed"

(dorsiflexed) and turned out (everted) to prepare for the propulsive

phase, which is an attempt to grab non-moving water and hold it

(put pressure on the bottom and inside of the foot). Again, be sure

not to combine this step with the previous one. Wait for the heels

to reach the butt before unpointing the toes.

7 Create a propulsive surge

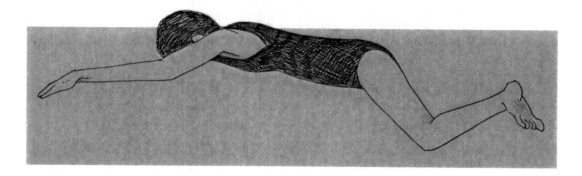

Rotate the feet outside the knees. Continue this rounded motion, feeling pressure on the insides of the lower legs and on the bottoms of the feet, until the legs come together for the glide. Yes, the lower leg kick relates to the lower arm stroke, each involving rotation outside a more stable upper limb.

Like all other skills, this one needs conscious performance of a single symmetrical kick until an optimal surge is created, perhaps using Drill **c.** first, and then from the glide position.

Cover progressively more distance from a push-off, recovering heels first, before an effective kick into a relaxed glide position.

8 Combine arm stroke and kick

Only after an effective arm stroke and an effective kick have been established separately should there be consideration of coordination and, even later, breathing.

After establishing the glide position, minimize the arm/hand motion at first while the heels recover and prepare to kick,

then squeeze the elbows during the whip kick into the glide.

The arms stroke while the heels recover, and the legs propel as the arms recover to the glide position.

9 Do no more than this single stroke

Master this **single** stroke from a push-off, a firm but relaxed arm movement followed by an effective kick surge and glide. Don't "kick the hands apart."

Kick into and hold the glide position, exaggerated by locking thumbs, if necessary.

Gradually widen the arm stroke during this one complete stroke without adding another, as per Rule Two.

10 Add breathing

Lift head, only slightly, to inhale early in the non-competitive stroke as hands separate, exhaling forcefully below the surface along with the propulsive drive of the whip kick. Think: **ARMS and BREATHE, KICK and GLIDE**.

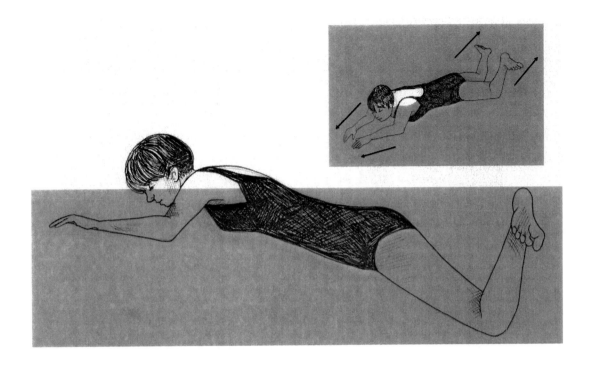

11 Progress to two strokes from a push-off, then gradually add more

Don't hurry this progression. Stop when rhythm is lost, rest, and start over from a push-off. A relaxed, rhythmic Breaststroke is the final result.

BREASTSTROKE DRILLS

a. An effective hand pitch can be developed most dramatically with a vertical sculling drill. The swimmer stays vertical in deep water, without kicking. Arms start straight together and stay straight as the hands scull out and in, like polishing a table.

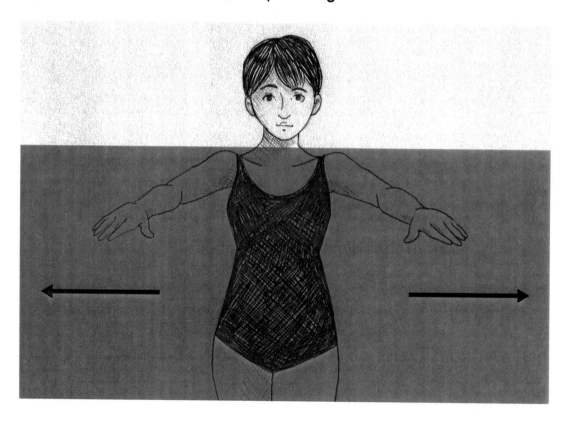

It surprises swimmers to find that they can, even with so much resistance and no backward motion, actually make forward progress in this position as they learn by trial and error the most effective hand pitch positions for pressing out and in.

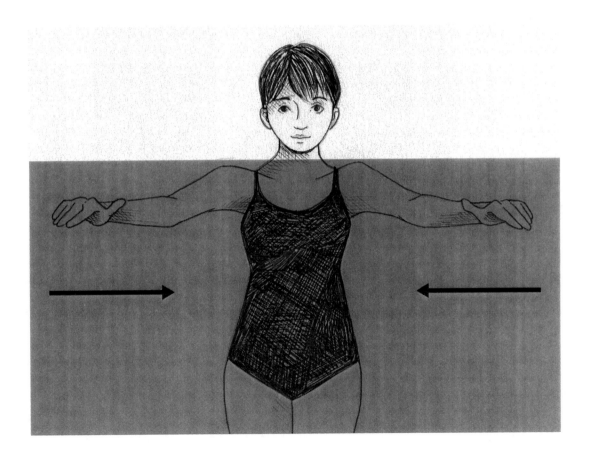

b. Arms alone with glide (Step 3).

c. Kick, holding the side of the pool with one hand on the pool edge or gutter, and the other hand, fingers pointing down, lower on the wall to lever and brace the body horizontally, legs extended together. Kick as from glide (Steps 5-7).

d. Vertical kicking. With arms and hands extended at side in deep water, sink below the surface while recovering heels. Then kick toward the bottom to return to the surface.

e. Legs alone with glide, arms extended in front.

f. Double kick (two kicks per arm stroke) with whole stroke to stress extended glide.

g. Measure progress. Count the number of strokes it takes to swim one length of the pool. This will establish a basis for comparison later on.

Butterfly Stroke

The Butterfly stroke is a prime example of Fundamental One because it was originated by breaststrokers who decreased resistance with an over-water recovery and increased propulsion with a longer application of arm-stroke force.

However, while the Butterfly developed from the Breaststroke, it is better considered as a Double-arm Crawl.

1 **Use the Push-Off & Glide (Page 15) to create momentum**

2 Establish the glide position for the stroke

The Butterfly glide position after the push-off is similar to that for the Breaststroke, a rotation to a prone position on the front by dropping the upper shoulder and hip.

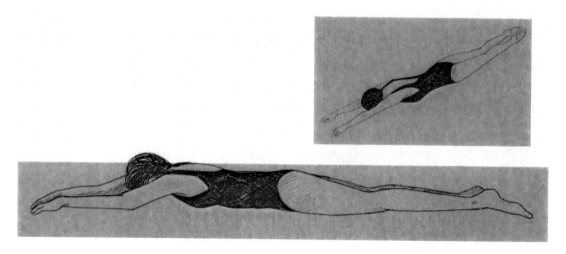

Keep the head and face in the water, but with arms and hands extended at approximately shoulder width. As in other strokes, the arms are angled slightly down for a deep catch, elbows up.

This relaxed stretch is the glide position for the Butterfly, to which it is vitally important that each stroke returns.

3 Develop a kick, but separately

Butterfly "dolphin" kicking is fun. It can be done any number of ways—on front or back or side, arms up or down, head in or out, using kickboard (conversational) or not. The author's preference is for kicking on the side, from the Crawl or Sidestroke glide position, switching left and right sides after each length, the same as for Crawl. Regardless, the kick originates from the hips, not the knees, with minimal knee bend, and the ankles should be kept loose.

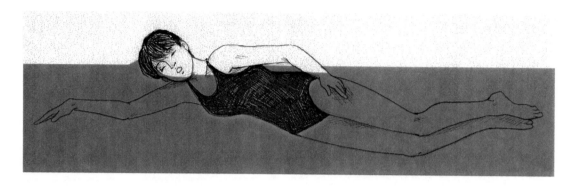

That being said, kicking is basically irrelevant to learning the stroke. A former Olympian known for his super-fast Fly kick once declared, "Butterfly is 90% arms," and that is best how to learn it.

The legs will follow if the arm stroke is effective, and eventually the kick can receive more emphasis.

4 Catch the water with high elbows

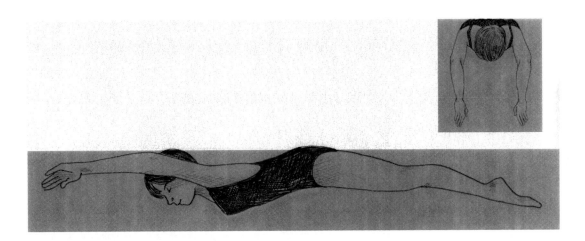

Start the arm stroke from an elbow-up, double-arm catch. The catch establishes a propulsive position with the hands and forearms anchored as if "over a barrel" to enable the body to move past.

5 Create a surge by levering the body past the anchored hands

Unlike swimming the Crawl, Butterfly swimmers can't roll to keep their lower arms and hands close to the body early in the stroke. Instead, from the catch, the hands and lower arms press out and slightly down against non-moving water.

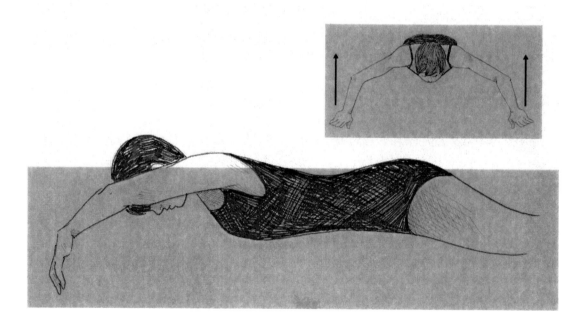

This is necessary for the swimmer to get the body past the anchored hands, which have to move out beyond shoulder width and then back in—still elbows-up—to finish, extended at the thighs.

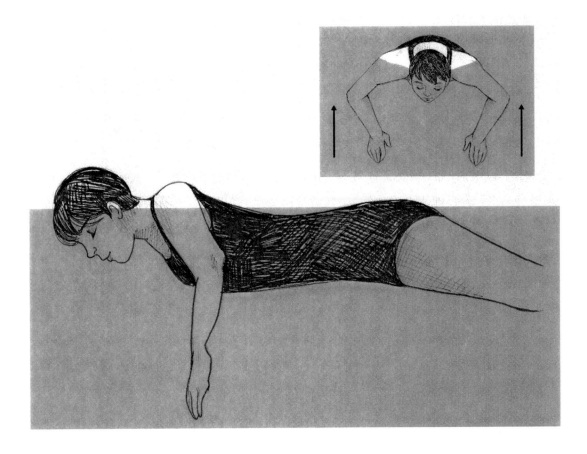

Not that it is immediately easy, but Rule Two calls for just a good push-off, glide, and a single stroke that finishes for now with thumbs at the thighs.

6 Finish the stroke cycle with the recovery to glide position

Having accomplished the push-off, glide, and one-arm stroke several times to generate an ever-increasing surge, the student's next step is to round off the momentum of the thigh-extended arms into an over-water recovery that finishes in the glide position.

The recovery should be relaxed, lifting the elbows just enough that the lower arms and hands are clear above the water surface.

7 Do no more than this single stroke

After a few repetitions of this complete arm stroke, the swimmer should focus on the finishing glide, particularly on waiting for the hips to rise. The arms returning to the glide position, angled down, will help the hips (by Newton's Third Law, around the body's center of buoyancy) to rise to the surface. Only then can the swimmer be ready for a second arm stroke.

8 Add a second stroke

The swimmer waits in the glide position for the hips to rise before initiating the second stroke, thus not attempting to "swim uphill." It is worth taking the practice time and adding the breathing to be comfortable with this rhythm and feel for the Butterfly.

9 Add breathing

For the same reasons as with non-competitive Breaststroke, the chin is lifted early in the stroke, only slightly, and dragged along the surface for inhalation as the arms widen, then dropped for forceful exhalation under water as the swimmer completes the propulsion and recovery.

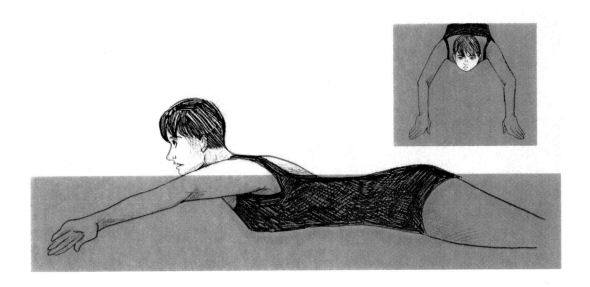

10 Add more strokes gradually

The key to advancing beyond two strokes is keeping the hips on the surface by momentum/glide and by gradually adding the kick. Without making a special effort, the swimmer will find a two-kick rhythm during each cycle of a relaxed, non-competitive stroke and recovery.

Keep Rule Two in mind and limit the number of strokes to only those that are efficient, then stop, rest, and begin again from another push-off. It may take a while before the swimmer can complete a pool length efficiently, but sticking to Rule Two is worth it.

BUTTERFLY DRILLS

a. Kick, preferably on the side (same as Crawl), switching sides after each length, thus always facing same side wall.

b. Single-arm stroking on the side with fly kick, like Crawl, breathing to the side, again switching sides after each pool length (always facing same side wall).

c. Arms alone, preferably without using a pull-buoy®, waiting for hips to rise.

d. Measure progress. Count the number of strokes it takes to swim one length of the pool. This will establish a basis for comparison later on.

Elementary Backstroke

Elementary Back is a stroke in which arms and legs propel together. This symmetry simplifies it and invites learning it early in the swimmer's stroke progression, before relearning the more difficult strokes.

Elementary Backstroke is ideal for learning/relearning the two phases common to all swim strokes—recovery and propulsion. It helps reinforce the concept of a gliding position between strokes, especially because there is no struggle to breathe.

1

Use the Push-Off & Glide (Page 15) to create momentum

2 Establish the glide position for the stroke

As the swimmer's momentum from the push-off and glide slows, the next step is to drop the top hip and shoulder to rotate onto the back while adding a long stroke with both arms.

Hands finish at the sides, thumbs on thighs, legs extended, head back (to keep the hips up for least body resistance), which establishes the glide position for the Elementary Backstroke, to which each stroke returns. Try this a few times, increasing the distance covered.

3 Recover both arms simultaneously

From the glide position, the swimmer recovers hands (fingers) up the sides of the body to the armpits, which will cause the swimmer's elbows to bend and drop.

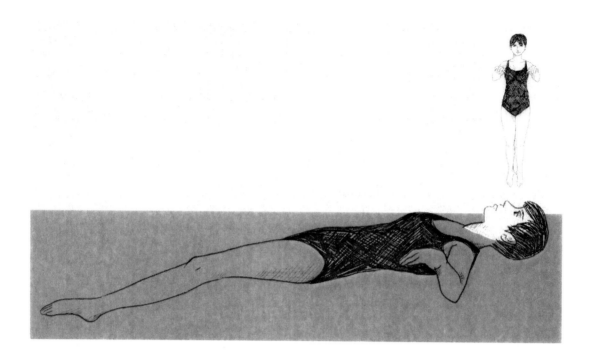

The second step is to leave the upper arms where they are while "shrugging" the shoulder blades together and extending the lower arms and hands outward, elbows down, to prepare for the propulsive phase.

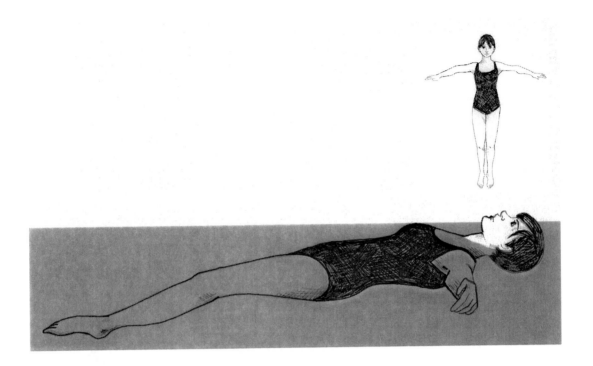

Together, these two moves constitute the recovery phase for the

Elementary Backstroke.

4 Create a surge

The swimmer "anchors" the hand/arm levers against the water to move the body past. The swimmer should feel pressure on the insides of the upper arms while attempting to, in effect, "throw" water toward the feet.

This creates a surge as the body passes the hands, which attempt to keep a steady pressure against the water without jerking.

This single-stroke skill needs to be repeated a few times to develop a more powerful surge.

5 Add a second stroke

Keeping the head back for the longest possible glide, the swimmer recovers, again minimizing resistance, with what should now have become a single movement (recovery phase) rather than the two distinct stages of Step 3. The surge (propulsive phase) may be increased with a little hand placement experimentation.

6 Add breathing

As with other strokes, inhalation takes place during the recovery phase, and a strong exhalation accompanies the propulsive phase.

7 Develop a kick, beginning with the recovery

The most difficult skill to learn for the Elementary Backstroke is the whip kick. Think **heels**. Two aspects are important here. One, recovering the heels first stresses bending at the knees and not at the hips; two, keeping the toes in line with the lower leg on recovery (not turned out) will prevent overstretching knee tendons

and ligaments, the source of painful "breaststroker's knee."

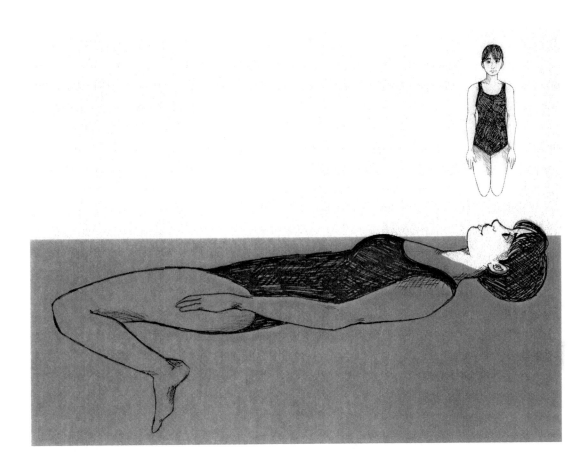

8 Prepare to kick by "catching" the water

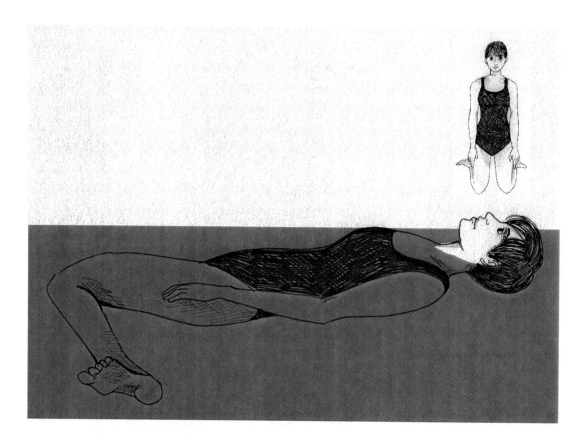

When the heels reach the butt, then toes can be "unpointed"

(dorsiflexed) and turned out (everted) to prepare for the propulsive phase, which is an attempt to grab non-moving water and hold it (put pressure on the bottom and inside of the foot).

Again, be sure **not** to combine this step with the previous one. Wait for the heels to reach the butt before unpointing the toes.

9 Create a propulsive surge

Rotate the feet outside the knees. Continue this rounded motion, feeling pressure on the insides of the lower legs and bottoms of the feet, until the legs come together for the glide.

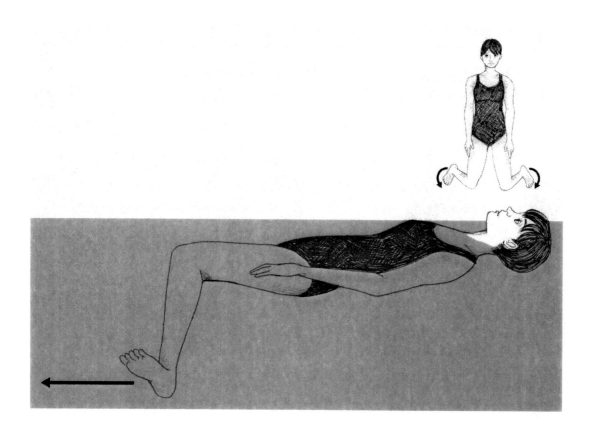

Like all other skills, this one needs conscious performance of a

single symmetrical kick until an optimal surge is created, perhaps

using Drill **b.** first, and then from the glide position.

10 Work on just a single effective kick

Use the same "1-2-3" for the leg movements as for the arms (Steps 7-9), again transitioning to a blend of the first two with **Recover** and **Kick**. Cover progressively more distance from a push-off, recovering heels first, before an effective kick into a relaxed glide position.

11 Add a second kick

Progress to a recovery from the glide position and a second effective kick. Incidentally, it's OK for knees, slightly apart, to break the surface a bit, but keep the head back.

12 Combine arm stroke and kick

Coordination should be considered only after an effective arm stroke and an effective kick have been established. From the glide position, the arms and legs recover and propel together with the same two-phase (Recover-Surge) rhythm developed separately.

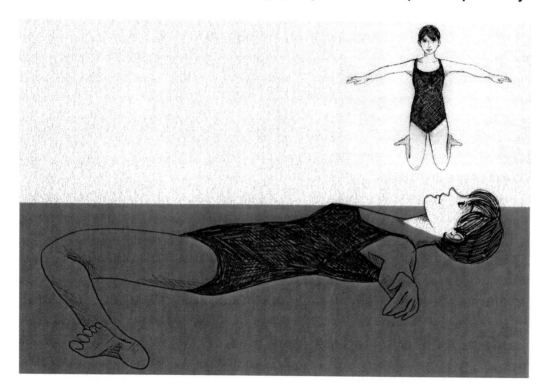

Be sure the head is back in the water to bring the hips up for least body resistance. Work on timing an optimal surge with a single stroke. Exhaling, if not already automatically simultaneous with the propulsive phase, can be included before adding a second complete stroke, and gradually more.

ELEMENTARY BACKSTROKE DRILLS

a. Vertical kicking. With arms and hands extended at side in deep water, sink below surface while recovering heels. Then kick toward the bottom to return to the surface.

b. Practice kick by working from the side of the pool (the wall at the swimmer's back), holding on to the gutter or deck with both arms.

c. Legs alone with glide, arms extended up or down.

d. Arms alone with glide.

e. Pole drill, described in section for Instructors.

f. Measure progress. Count the number of strokes it takes to swim one length of the pool. This will establish a basis for comparison later on.

Sidestroke

The Sidestroke is a relaxing stroke, a strong coordination of arms and kick for propulsion, followed by a long and restful glide. A strong kick is essential for swimmers who later opt for lifeguard training.

1 **Use the Push-Off & Glide (Page 15) to create momentum**

2 **Use an effective arm stroke to establish the glide position for the stroke**

As the swimmer's momentum from the push-off and glide slows, the next step is to add a long stroke with the top arm (elbow up, with hand "catching" the water below the surface, as if over a

barrel, to "anchor" the hand/arm lever as the body moves past it).

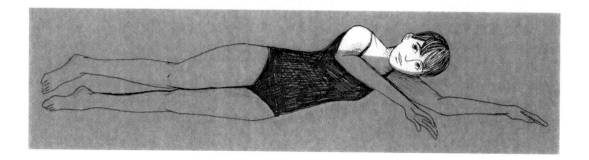

The swimmer should feel a surge as the body passes the hand

and top arm, which attempt to keep a steady pressure against the

water without jerking the "barrel" or slipping off it.

The body stays close to the hand, which finishes at the side,

thumb on thigh, to establish the glide position for the Sidestroke.

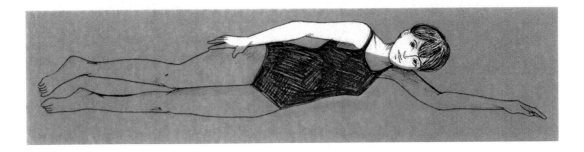

The bottom or lead arm should be angled slightly downward for a variety of reasons (less shoulder tension, less tendency to move hand toward the surface and thus increase resistance, better angle to apply propulsive force).

3 Stick to this single skill

This basic skill needs to be repeated a few times to develop a more powerful surge. Then do the same on the other side, still just the push-off and glide, followed by the top arm stroke and glide, with bottom arm leading, top arm extended, thumb on thigh, legs extended together, and head in the water to keep the hips up for least body resistance.

4 Recover and stroke with both arms

Next, use both arms from the glide position. There are two phases, recovery and propulsion. Recover the top arm, elbow up, by dragging the thumb along the body.

At the same time, use the forearm and hand of the bottom (leading) arm to "scoop" toward the chin. Minimize this at first, then gradually increase the depth of the "scoop" until hands come together in front of the chin.

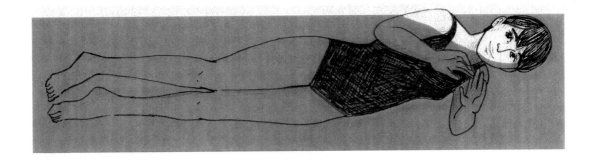

The second phase consists of the same top arm stroke that established the glide position, simultaneous with extension of the bottom arm into the glide position. Use no kick, or use a slight flutter for balance, being sure to keep the head in the water.

Do just this one stroke of the arms to get the surge right, several times, and then repeat it to get two good propulsions on one side before doing the same progression on the other side.

5 Develop a kick, beginning with the recovery

Think **heels**. For recovery, from glide position, focus first on recovering heels to the butt, knees together. Keep heels in line with spine.

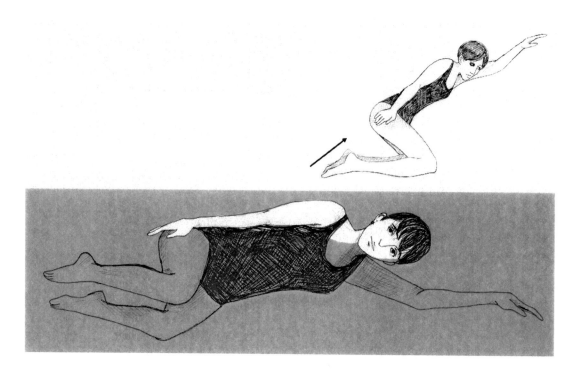

6 Prepare to kick by "catching" the water

When the heels reach the butt, then toes can be pointed as the

bent legs separate **horizontally**, top leg forward and bottom leg

back. The top leg is usually not a problem. It's the bottom

thigh/knee that needs to separate horizontally, not vertically, to open the scissors for optimal effect.

7 Create a surge

In one smooth motion, straighten both legs horizontally and bring them together forcefully. Stress this surge provided by the scissoring action of the kick.

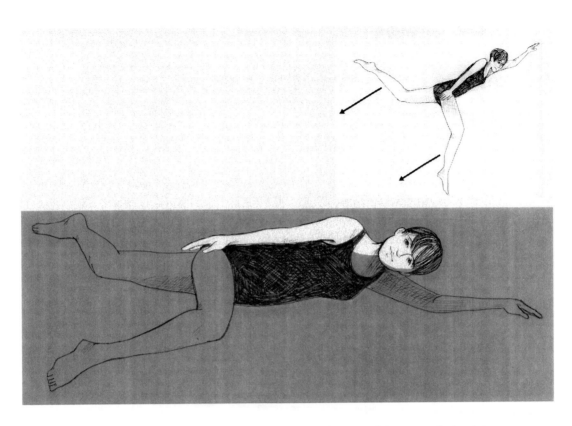

After the propulsive effort, hold the glide position, pointed toes

overlapping to keep from crossing past each other. If any part of

the sequence in Steps 5-7 proves difficult, try first using Drill **b**.

8 Work on just a single effective kick before progressing

Kick from the glide position after push-off and initial arm stroke, or just push off in the glide position. As always, just one good kick, covering progressively more distance into a relaxed glide position, with the head in the water on the lead shoulder. Then add a second kick.

9 Repeat the progression on the other side

Hopefully, one side will be both more effective and more comfortable than the other.

10 Combine arms and legs and breathing

Recover the legs as the arms come together from the glide

position.

The propulsive phase combines the kick with the elbow-up stroke

of the top arm, while the bottom arm is extended slightly

downward, as if into a sleeve.

Exhaling, if not already automatically simultaneous with the propulsive phase, can be included and practiced with the complete stroke, increasing the distance covered, before adding a second complete stroke, and gradually more.

SIDESTROKE DRILLS

a. Arms alone with glide.

b. Legs alone on wall (Steps 5-7) —Sidestroke kicking on the wall is done with the hand of the top arm holding the deck or gutter. The bottom-arm hand, fingers pointed down, braces the body, and extends it horizontally out from the wall to prepare for the "scissor" kick.

c. Legs alone with glide.

d. Measure progress. Count the number of strokes it takes to swim one length of the pool. This will establish a basis for comparison later on.

Turns

Efficient turns are characteristic of proficient swimmers. The Getting Started chapter indicates that all strokes begin the same way, which also means that they have in common the second part of an open, non-competitive turn.

Instead of considering different, stroke-specific turns, the swimmer needs only to learn the approach to the pool wall and reversal for each stroke that puts the swimmer into the common push-off position that presents the least resistance.

1 All turns can be learned together

The turns for all strokes follow the same pattern with most elements (**reach and touch, reverse and breathe, plant and sink, push off and glide**), so it makes sense to learn them in a single pool session or two.

2 Begin first with the Crawl turn

The swimmer has already been Getting Started on both sides, using the common push-off to begin each stroke. This becomes particularly helpful for the Crawl Stroke turn because the swimmer needs to be able to use whichever hand happens to glide into the wall.

The glide position for the Crawl puts the trailing arm at the swimmer's side, where it stays pointing at the opposite wall, while the swimmer's momentum brings the knees, feet, and torso toward the wall, to be placed in the usual position for pushing off.

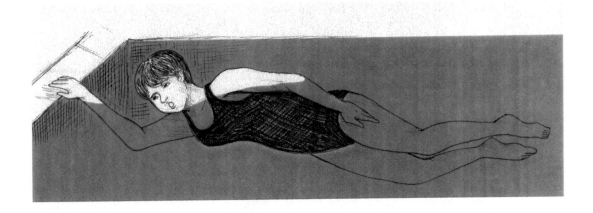

That's it—a relaxed glide into the wall, a breath taken while the body reverses itself, planting the feet while sinking (same as Step

3 on Page 17) and extending both arms, and then the usual push-off and glide.

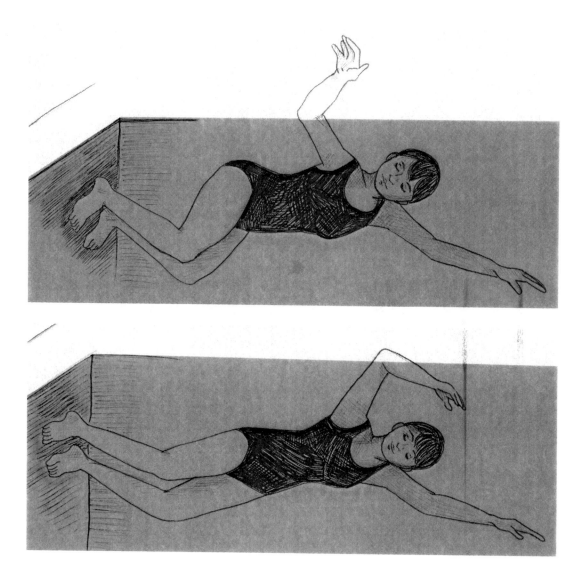

3 Practice until the total movement becomes efficient

Practice on both sides, and the resulting smooth rhythm should carry over for the other strokes.

There is one Crawl Stroke adjustment to be made now after the push-off and glide. Whereas the swimmer first learned to start stroking with the top arm (the better to learn to keep the elbow up and to establish the proper Crawl glide positioning with only a single arm), **the swimmer now should stroke first with the bottom arm**, which more efficiently initiates the stroke rotation to its glide position on the other side.

4 Learn next to turn on the back

The Back Crawl turn works the same way, regardless of which hand glides into the wall. The other hand is left behind while the body reverses and sinks, the legs bending to place the feet (pointing to the side) for the push-off. And again, it is more efficient to begin stroking with the bottom arm.

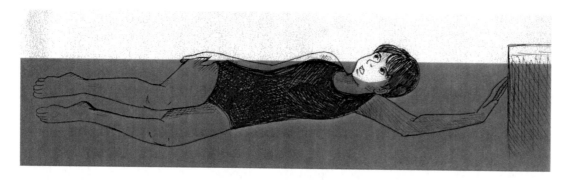

The Elementary Backstroke turn works like the Back Crawl, with the swimmer choosing one arm to reach back, rotating to that side while approaching the wall.

5 Next, turn when on the front

The Breaststroke and Butterfly turns are both performed in the same way. As the swimmer approaches the wall with both arms extended in the glide position, one arm can be dropped behind (this is not competitive swimming) while the body reverses to the other side as it does for the Crawl turn.

6 Sidestroke turns are unique

The swimmer who wishes to continue on the same side after the turn needs to reach for the wall with the **top** (non-leading) arm, dropping the lead arm to help reverse the body into the proper push-off position for continuing.

7 Finally, there is the flip turn

The Crawl flip turn reverses direction in a faster way. Like the others, it is a 180° turn, 90° of which occurs on the push-off. All the "flip" contributes is the other 90° without taking a breath.

All flip turns are the same, regardless of the swimmer's lead arm. The next-to-last stroking arm is not recovered but kept at the swimmer's side in the glide position, to be joined by the other arm at its side as the final stroke is taken before the turn. Thus, both arms remain at the swimmer's sides, shoulders square, elbows in, palms down, with little fingers touching thighs before the "flip" is initiated.

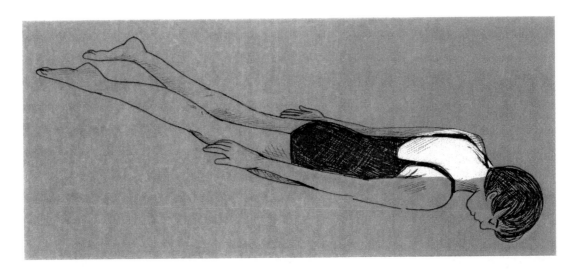

For safety, learn the flip turn well away from the wall at first.

The swimmer needs some momentum from the wall, from the pool bottom, or just from a double-arm stroke, after which the body lies prone (on the stomach) with arms at sides as described above.

The "flip" is performed by pushing the hands toward the pool bottom to lift the hips, which can be aided by a butterfly kick, while ducking the chin and shoulders (square to the wall) and folding the body in the middle, the hands coming together in front of the face.

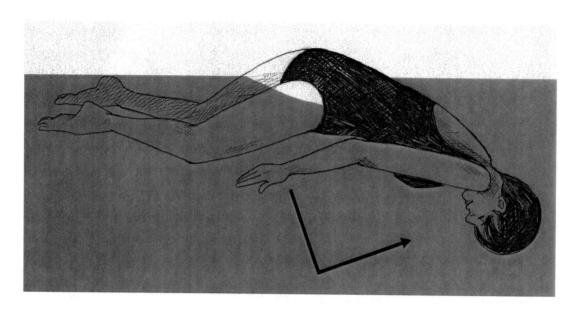

It is important throughout to keep both elbows close to the body, not "crucifying" the turn. The momentum generated will carry the legs over the upper body, resulting in the swimmer being on the back or side, whichever is natural.

The eventual goal, of course, is a push-off on one side. Thus, if the swimmer has a natural imbalance that results in being on one side, that's fine. However, if the flip is so naturally balanced that the result is a somersault onto the back, this can be "corrected" by touching one hand to the top of the head during the flip, experimenting until one hand or the other feels more comfortable in producing the desired result.

Once the swimmer feels efficient with this heels-over-head movement, the flip turn can be performed closer and closer to the wall, but never so close as to flip the feet onto the deck or gutter or too high on the wall.

Obviously, judging distance from the wall is made easier with lanes ending in a "T" on the pool bottom, but the swimmer by this point will have enough experience to make the needed adjustments to plant the feet for an optimal push-off.

Good swimmers make good turns. Be sure to add the icing of efficient turns on the cake of efficient swimming.

Instructing Better Swimming

A conversation with a student from many years back:

"It's no use, Bob. I can't get it. I don't even feel like I'm doing anything."

"Did you count your strokes for that lap, Mindy?"

"Of course. 22."

"And how many do you usually take?"

"28-29."

"So you're swimming the same distance, with less effort, and half a dozen fewer strokes?"

"Omigosh! You mean I did it? Omigosh, I don't believe I finally did it!"

Moments of epiphany like this are among a swim instructor's best rewards, and the purpose of *Swim Better*.

Getting Started

Regardless of stroke and regardless of time available, I recommend that every program of instruction start off the same way, with a push-off and glide. It is the essence of what this book is about.

Over my many years of teaching, I have found that the clearest indicator of students' swimming efficiency is simply to have them swim into and away from a wall. Most swimmers make a mess of any stroke and "open" turn, and they can feel their own inefficiency. They fumble with their hands and push off on their stomachs with their heads out of the water. So that's the starting point for doing something different (Rule 1) and for doing only what is successful (Rule 2).

To compare the efficiency of gliding/swimming on the front or back with gliding/swimming on one side (something different), the instructor can demonstrate with a one- or two-foot piece of 2x4. Push it first under water with its flat sides on the top and bottom. It will quickly meet resistance and pop to the surface right away, unless it is pushed downward, in which case it will meet resistance and stop altogether. If instead the 2x4 is turned ninety degrees to be on its side, it will glide much farther under water, thus clearly making the instructor's point.

1   Begin at the pool wall

For teaching, here's how it goes. The students line up on the wall, facing the instructor at the end of the pool, with one hand (arbitrarily, let's use the right) on the gutter or pool's edge, feet together on the wall a foot or two below the surface and pointing toward the instructor, knees bent, with left arm and hand stretched out toward the opposite wall to the instructor's right. ("Knees, toes, and nose pointed at me.")

2   First movement: release and LIFT the arm

That's it. Just release and lift and let the body sink. Simple action, but it won't happen for everybody. Even if there are 30 students lined up on a 75-foot wall, it will be easy to see those who reach instead of just lifting and/or those who automatically extend their legs and start pushing off the wall.

The instructor needs to get everyone back on the wall and wait until they are again in the proper position before repeating the action. This needs to be done only two or three times because it will be repeated continually as Getting Started progresses and as strokes are developed.

3 READY - lift and, while sinking, extend the right arm to meet the left—hand over hand

Again, that's it, and again there will be those who will not just pause and relax (the key to everything) during and after this simple action, and it will need to be repeated (again only once or twice) to "get everyone on the same page."

All the while, the instructor has established the most useful teacher-student positioning, as well as establishing attention and discipline, the preference for quality over quantity, and also the initial steps toward trust. This overall movement of lifting, sinking, and extending hand-over-hand ("ears between the upper arms"), while maintaining feet on the wall, is now Step One (**READY**) of the teaching progression.

4 GO - Extend the legs and push off under water, with the body stretched as long as possible on its side to produce a long glide

This will need to be repeated so that glides can get farther and farther from the wall. With the instructor's suggestion, students can experiment and adjust the depth of their feet on the wall and/or the angle of their bent knees (ninety degrees is optimal) to get more push for gliding distance.

Students who maintain one hand on top of the other can take optimal advantage of the longest possible waterline. Once again, that's it; nothing else. Depending on the number of students in the class, the push-offs may have to be done in wave or group formation (see Appendix) to avoid collisions.

5 Repeat these steps on the other side, holding on to the wall or gutter with the left hand

Next, now that all students have established a long underwater glide from one side of the pool, the instructor can have the students proceed from the end of their glide to the other side of the pool. If, instead, they have been using the end of the pool, then only the instructor need move to the other side. Either way, the students can now face the instructor with their left hands holding on to the wall or gutter, and the process (**READY** Pause **GO**) can be repeated on this other side. Certainly, it should take less time, but again the instructor needs to be assured that students have the discipline to do only the action(s) called for.

At this point the instructor has established the first skill toward efficient swimming. Pausing long enough to sink, placing feet on the wall a little higher or lower, pushing through the chest, keeping a dynamic balance, and developing the longest-possible glide on both sides, are, all together, more than enough for a swimmer to work on before adding specific stroke elements.

I have spent time and detail here to be sure that the instructor uses the **Fundamentals** and **Rules** for this vital lesson, something different from what students have done before. Not only that, but they and their instructor have utilized important bits of physics: minimizing resistance by pushing off under water, avoiding surface tension, and lengthening the "water line," as well as Newton's Third Law of Motion, where the action of raising the arm from the pool's edge creates a reaction that helps the body to sink for the most efficient push-off.

And, most important, the instructor has established discipline, instituted a teaching/learning pattern, and used success to create trust.

Everything that follows is devoted to building on this start.

Stroking

Efficient and effective stroking requires efficient and effective instruction, too. *Swim Better* assumes the instructor's familiarity with the strokes and the basics common to all strokes—head in water, glide, two phases, deep catch, stroking for distance, etc.

It assumes, too, that our common goal as instructors is developing strokes that look and feel right, and all of us can make use of tips and cues toward enhanced instruction. We are results-oriented, and my purpose here is to show instructors both the *how* and the *why* of efficient stroke mechanics.

The instructor, after teaching the push-off and glide, controls progress in each stroke, establishing a glide position, creating a force that propels the swimmer's body past its anchored extremities, and developing for the individual or group just a single efficient and effective stroke.

Focusing on quality rather than quantity will motivate students to make drills a regular part of every lesson or workout. For **re**learners, especially, stroke mechanics are more important than conditioning (swimming laps) and avoiding the risk of returning to old habits. As a coaching phrase goes, "It's not the yards in the workout, but the workout in the yards that counts." This cannot be stressed enough to both instructors and swimmers.

As for stroke order, there are several factors involved in choosing how many and which strokes to teach. If there is sufficient time for several, the instructor will need to consider the order in which they are taught effectively. For instance, it can mean delaying instruction for the Crawl Stroke. As a long-term example of Rule 1, before attempting a relearned Crawl Stroke, the swimmer may need to build up a sufficient vocabulary of efficient skills that are transferable to the Crawl. This can be done by working first on another stroke or a progression of other strokes.

Elementary Backstroke is as different as possible from the struggles of an inefficient Crawl Stroke. It is simple and relaxed, performed on the back to negate any breathing concerns, and the arms and legs propel together. Yet it does stress stroke length and includes a bent-elbow arm stroke. Thus it is a good first stroke if the instructor has the time available, such as in a semester-long course.

With less time, or time enough for just one stroke other than Crawl, or just the need to use something different as a transition to relearning, Sidestroke is ideal for getting away from bad habits while developing a transferable glide position and effective propulsion from a bent-elbow arm stroke, as well as a relaxed stroke with no struggle to breathe.

Incidentally, most competitive swimmers have never learned either of these two strokes and can benefit from the instruction, certainly if they eventually enroll in a Lifeguarding course.

As another example, Back Crawl, because so many elements carry over to Crawl with minimal concern for breathing, may well precede Crawl in the teaching progression.

Most of all, though, the instructor's own comfort with specific strokes will be the prime factor in determining stroke order. Each stroke can transfer to others from principles and positions already learned, and these are noted specifically for each stroke. Creativity and imagination go a long way as the instructor develops transitions from one efficient stroke to help students learn the next one.

Finally, don't skip any steps or combine any as you work on each stroke, even if a step takes just a few minutes. Instructor discipline is as important as is self-discipline to the relearner.

Instructing Specific Strokes & Turns

Just as the push-off and glide in the chapter on Getting Started fit all strokes, progress in each stroke follows a simple pattern for the instructor.

First is establishing a glide position for that specific stroke, especially one not previously familiar to the swimmer. Second is creating a force that propels the swimmer's body past its anchored extremities. These are the two aspects of Fundamental One, decreasing resistance and increasing propulsion. Last, adhering to Rule 2, is an insistence on developing for the individual or group just a single efficient and effective stroke before any attempt at further progress.

Additionally, there are specific stroke-related drills that are better taught by a competent instructor than left to self-instruction. Teaching principles related to specific strokes, and elements helpful to progressing from one specific stroke to another, are included, too, as suggestions for the instructor, along with room to add more.

Crawl Stroke

It pains me to watch swimmers struggle with the Crawl, not so much swimming a pool length as beating it to death—taking as many as 40+ strokes for 25 yards—when I've seen relaxed champions warm up by using as few as ten. The Crawl Stroke thus can be as efficient as the primarily gliding strokes if it is **re**learned in a similar fashion through an instructor.

This is the perfect application of Rule 1 and what *Swim Better* is all about. If swimmers and instructors were asked to demonstrate the glide position for the Crawl Stroke, probably 98% of them would use the Breaststroke glide position, on the stomach with both arms stretched in front. Being on the side with the bottom arm leading and the top arm down at the swimmer's side is truly different, and makes it more difficult for the swimmer to revert to the formerly less efficient stroke.

The instructor should observe the swimmers to determine the time to be spent on each unhurried step and drills.

The instructor's focus is on developing a long body position (glide) initiated by a strong push-off, maintained by a relaxed kick, and sustained by single-arm stroking with a focus on anchoring the hand and arm to lever the body past. Only when this has been achieved separately on each side does the stroke come together with a ten-kicks-and-switch rhythm that focuses on an alternating extended position, later reducing the number of kicks on each side (ten to six to three) into a normal six-beat crawl.

My favorite drill for teaching the Crawl is Jack Nelson's rope drill. With a rope tied to the hooks normally used for lane dividers or to steps a couple of feet below the surface, or even just across the pool for a stroke or two, one can simulate stroke length. Without kicking, the swimmer reaches as far forward as possible with **elbow up** to grasp the rope **with thumb pointing toward the swimmer.**

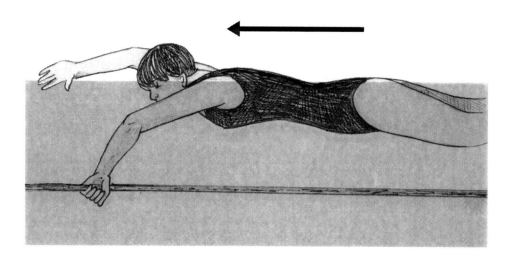

Then, keeping the elbow up, the swimmer pulls the body ("straddling" over the rope) past the hand, extending the hand as far backwards as possible before letting go and riding the momentum as far as possible before repeating with the opposite hand.

Swimmers can try to see how few "strokes" are needed to go one pool length on the rope and then return by trying to duplicate the same rhythm without the rope. This rope drill can even benefit beginning swimmers, who develop right away the feeling of anchoring the hand and moving the body past it, thus learning the concepts of stroke length and glide from the first.

Another favorite drill is stroking with a closed hand, which eliminates pressure on the hand and forces the swimmer instead to use cues from the lower and upper arm. To swim with fists and then to open one's hands is greatly to heighten their sense of feel and ability to maintain the traction

necessary to propel the body past the hands. Scott Lemley's Fistgloves®
are a product designed to serve this purpose even more effectively.

Pressing up and out of the water, using the pool deck, as described in the
section on instructing Butterfly, can help to demonstrate the use of
effective elbow-up leverage.

Crawl Teaching Principles

- Remind students of the high-energy cost of kicking, meaning thus to
  kick not so much for propulsion as for body position and balance.
- Use an excessive kicking count between arm strokes at first to
  emphasize extension and glide.
- Use an excessive body roll at first to help with the switch emphasis
  and to facilitate recovery.
- Elbow is always above hand, throughout stroke and recovery.
- Recover by lifting elbow first, then letting lower arm hang and
  fingertips drag on surface; relaxed downward entry, deep catch; finish
  with thumb at thigh.

Elements to use in teaching Crawl from/toward other Strokes

- Glide position (Sidestroke, Back Crawl)
- Bent elbow (Elementary Back, Back [Inverted] Crawl, Sidestroke)
- Flutter kick (Back Crawl)
- Two-phase side-to-side alternation (Back Crawl)
- Single-Arm and Switch drills (Back Crawl)

Back Crawl Stroke

The instructor's most important role in teaching the Back Crawl is to help swimmers understand and apply the concept that Back Crawl is not swum on the back, but **through** the back, alternating side-to-side.

The instructor should follow the steps to learning the Back Crawl Stroke in the Better Swimming section, using observation of the swimmers to determine the time to be spent on each unhurried step and drills.

The instructor's focus is on keeping the head and spine in line without being directly on the back, rather alternating sides **through** the back to develop a comfortable ten-kicks-and-switch rhythm that focuses on an alternating extended position and then reduces the number of kicks on each side (ten to six to three) into a normal six beats per cycle.

My favorite drill for teaching the Back Crawl is the perfect affirmation of Fundamental B. It uses a pole held by the instructor vertically against the bottom about three or four feet off the wall.

The first of a line of swimmers along the wall lies in glide position next to the wall with lead arm extended, grasping the pole about a foot underwater.

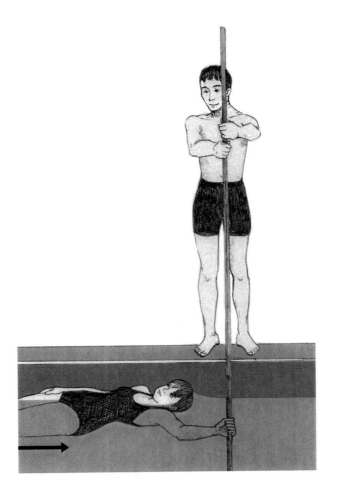

The swimmer then uses the pole to propel the body past the anchored pole (Fundamental B) to get the feel of an effective backstroke. After the line of swimmers has performed this, the instructor starts the line again with the pole anchored closer to the wall.

By continuing in this fashion, swimmers are forced to develop a body roll and become more fish-like in order to propel themselves past the pole on their side. Of course, the entire procedure is then repeated with swimmers facing the opposite direction to use the pole on their other side.

Back Crawl Teaching Principles

- Remind students of the high-energy cost of kicking, meaning thus to kick not so much for propulsion as for body position and balance.
- Use an excessive kicking count between arm strokes at first to emphasize extension and glide.
- Use an excessive body roll at first to help with the switch emphasis and to facilitate recovery, rotating the shoulders and hips on the long body axis, but keeping the head steady and on line **in the water**.
- Recover by lifting thumb first, rotate recovering arm to enter with little finger first; deep drive into catch, finish thumb at thigh with palm down to elevate shoulder for recovery.

Elements to use in teaching Back Crawl from/toward other Strokes

- Glide position (Sidestroke, Crawl)
- Bent elbow (Elementary Back, Crawl, Sidestroke)
- Flutter kick (Crawl)
- Two-phase side-to-side alternation (Crawl)
- Single-Arm and Switch drills (Crawl)

Breaststroke

Like the other strokes, Breaststroke can be taught first in order, but it might better follow the Elementary Backstroke, where the whip kick and glide can be taught without concern for breathing.

The instructor should follow the steps to learning the Breaststroke in the Better Swimming section, using observation of the swimmers to determine the time to be spent on each unhurried step and drills.

The instructor's focus is on a comfortable **arms-and-breathe**, **kick-and-glide** rhythm.

Doc Counsilman used a drill to combine arms and breathing by having swimmers lie extended face down in the water with arms extended and their feet hooked on the deck or gutter. He would have them move just hands and arms out and down to discover that by Newton's Third Law of Motion their bodies would rise.

Then, keeping the arms together, he would have them lift their heads to discover that by the same Law their bodies would sink. Therefore, they could see that a simultaneous head lift and arm stroke counter each other and reduce up-and-down body movement.

Breaststroke Teaching Principles

- Stress the relaxed nature of a non-competitive stroke.
- Focus on the two-phase rhythm: arms and breathe, kick and glide.
- Don't let the swimmer "kick the hands apart." Having swimmers end their arm recovery with thumbs locked together will force them to kick into the glide position and hold it.

Elements to use in teaching Breaststroke from/toward other Strokes

- Bilateral symmetry (Elementary Back, Butterfly)
- Recover heels first (Side, Elementary Back)
- Unpoint toes (dorsiflexion), rotate feet outside knees (Elementary Back)
- Propulsive pressure on bottom & inside of feet (Elementary Back)
- Stroke with elbow above hand (Crawl, Butterfly, Side)
- Hands never meet below chin (Side)
- Exhale with propulsive leg phase (Elementary Back, Side)
- Inhale early in stroke (Butterfly)

Butterfly Stroke

Teaching the Butterfly well was most challenging to me for many years. My aspiration recalled a quotation from C.W. Ceram: "Genius is the ability to reduce the complicated to the simple," and also one from Thomas Edison: "Genius is 1% inspiration and 99% perspiration." I spent years of study, observation, and experimentation attempting to find the easiest way of teaching the stroke, just to be able to say, simply, "Do this." The result is the chapter on Butterfly in the Better Swimming section of this book.

Teaching "Fly" is probably approached best after the Crawl, but nevertheless it is possible even to be taught first if—or when—circumstances warrant. The instructor should follow the steps to learning the Butterfly stroke in the Better Swimming section, using observation of the swimmers to determine the time to be spent on each unhurried step and drills.

The instructor's focus is on a double-arm Crawl Stroke, applied only when the hips are up.

The lack of understanding Fundamental B is responsible for some of the terrible gyrations I've seen when swimmers, as they have been instructed, attempt artificially to create a "keyhole" as they pull their hands past their bodies.

The problem to solve, instead, is getting the shoulders past the hands. Having the student, facing the wall in deep water, reach up and attempt to press up and out of the water using the pool deck will illustrate the need to place hands and arms outside the shoulders, elbows up, for effective leverage.

Similarly, in the Butterfly, only after the head and shoulders are propelled past the hands can there be a propulsive, elbows-up "insweep." The sequence of outsweep and insweep, moving the body past anchored hands, is much simpler for the swimmer to understand and attempt than a "keyhole" analogy.

Butterfly Teaching Principles

- Remember that the glide position for Butterfly is with arms at shoulder width, the better for an effective elbows-up outsweep.
- Effective Butterfly stroking happens when the hips are at the surface. Early on, the swimmer must wait for hips to rise before initiating the arm stroke.
- Treat the stroke as a Double-arm Crawl.
- Repeating the push-off, glide, and two-stroke sequence, I have found, is enough to teach the rhythm and feel for Butterfly. Do that a lot before attempting more.

Elements to use in teaching Butterfly from/toward other Strokes

- Bilateral symmetry (Breast, Elementary Back)
- Stroke with bent elbow (Back Crawl, Crawl, Breast, Elementary Back, Side)
- Inhale early in stroke (Breast)

Elementary Backstroke

Symmetry simplifies it and invites the instructor to make early use of it in the stroke-teaching progression. It is ideal for teaching or **re**-teaching the two phases—recovery and propulsion—common to all swim strokes. It is also ideal for reinforcing the concept of a gliding position between strokes, especially without any struggle to breathe.

The instructor should follow the steps to learning the Elementary Backstroke in the Better Swimming section, using observation of the swimmers to determine the time to be spent on each step and its drills.

Instructors may want to teach Elementary Back arm movements first from a standing position in shallow water. Use a "1-2-3" count **UP-OUT-STROKE** to keep a large group together, sooner or later blending the "1" and "2" to use **RECOVER** and **STROKE** commands. The goal here is just one good recovery, arm stroke, and glide to get the surge right, and only then repeat for two good propulsions.

A forceful exhalation coordinated with the propulsive surge can be taught at this point or emphasized later with the overall coordination of arms and legs.

Obviously, the most difficult task to teach is the whip kick, particularly for swimmers who have made a habit of a less than efficient kick on back or front. Once the arm stroke and the leg kick have been learned separately, the instructor can have students stand in shallow water to combine them, using one leg at a time with the arms and breathing.

Elementary Backstroke Teaching Principles

- Be sure swimmers keep their heads back in the water to reduce resistance.
- Focus on arm movements first. Even with a light flutter kick or no kick at all, it is a relaxing stroke.
- Focus on the heels/feet when teaching the kick. Remember that the knees don't have to be together, nor do they have to be under water; they can break the surface slightly.
- Stress the rotation of the heels around the knees for an effective kick.
- Non-purists can allow students to recover arms above shoulder level. They can also teach arm movement or allow arms-alone drills with a flutter kick to maintain a level body position.

Elements to use in teaching Elementary Backstroke from/toward other Strokes

- Bilateral symmetry (Breast, Butterfly)
- Arms and legs propel together (Side)
- Recover heels first (Side, Breast)
- Unpoint toes (dorsiflexion), rotate feet around knees (Breast)
- Propulsive pressure from inside and bottom of feet (Breast)
- Recover arms close to body (Side)
- Stroke with bent elbow (Back Crawl, Crawl, Butterfly)
- Finish with thumb on thigh (Side, Back Crawl, Crawl)
- Exhale with propulsive phase (Side)

Sidestroke

The Sidestroke is excellent for instructing swimmers to use their extremities to "grip" the water and create a coordinated surge that propels the body into a long and relaxed glide. The instructor should follow the steps to learning the Sidestroke in the Better Swimming section, using observation of the swimmers to determine the time to be spent on each unhurried step and drills.

The instructor's focus is on the coordination of the top (stroking) arm with the propulsive scissor kick into a long glide.

More than likely, the instructor will have to bring students on deck for kick practice to increase horizontal thigh separation while preventing vertical separation of knees. Practice on both sides, although one side will probably be easier for each swimmer.

A deck (or shallow water standing) drill will probably be needed to teach two-phase coordination first, before adding arms to the kick from glide position in the water. Stand in "statue of liberty" glide position before recovering the top arm and top leg along with "scooping" the lead arm to prepare for the propulsive phase that includes extending the lead or bottom arm.

As always, work the proper timing on both sides. You may want also to include breath exhalation here with the propulsive phase.

Sidestroke Teaching Principles

- Be sure that the swimmer recognizes/identifies the glide position ("statue of liberty" analogy) to which each stroke returns.
- Stress moving the body past the hand, having the student "anchor" the hand/arm lever as the body moves past it.
- If the swimmer's head bobs, it is caused by vertical knee separation. Horizontal separation is necessary for an optimal "scissor" kick.
- Develop one good stroke (after push-off and glide position) on each side. Include breathing, exhaling on the propulsive phase. Use the pool lengthwise from the shallow end wall when adding a second good stroke.
- Two good strokes are enough for now.
- The non-purist instructor might possibly add attempts at an inverted kick on both sides for each student to pick the best of four combinations for comfort and power.

Elements to use in teaching Sidestroke from/toward other Strokes

- Glide position (Crawl, Back Crawl)
- Top arm and legs propel together (Elementary Back)
- Elbow up for stroking arm (Crawl)
- Finish with thumb on thigh (Elementary Back, Back Crawl, Crawl)
- Recover arms close to body (Elementary Back)
- Hands meet at upper chest, under chin (Breast)
- Recover heels first (Elementary Back, Breast)
- Exhale with propulsive phase (Elementary Back)

Turns

Instead of considering different, stroke-specific turns, the instructor who has started off all strokes the same way need only teach the approach to the pool wall and reversal for each stroke that puts the swimmer into the already-learned common push-off position that presents the least resistance.

The instructor has two options for teaching turns—to teach a turn with each stroke or to teach them all together in one or two lessons. I recommend the latter for a couple of reasons. First, there is really no need for turning at the stage where each stroke is learned or relearned, quality (one or a few good strokes) being the dominant factor over quantity.

Second, turning is a concept in itself, especially when the turns for all strokes follow a pattern with most elements the same (**reach and touch, reverse and breathe, plant and sink, push off and glide**), so it makes more sense to teach them all together.

The instructor should follow the steps to learning turns in the Better Swimming section. As with the push-off and the strokes, turns should be taught in a few small steps that every student can do correctly before moving on together.

The flip turn is included for two reasons: 1. Like the Butterfly stroke, this is a skill that even noncompetitive swimmers want to learn, if only for the fun of it. 2. The swimmer is already familiar with a good push-off, having used it for every stroke and most drills. The swimmer will have added an efficient open turn by this point, which is no more than adding a couple of elements, one at a time, to the push-off.

All that is required for the Crawl flip turn is to reverse direction in a new (and faster) way, again ending in the same push-off position learned in Getting Started, toes pointing to the side.

And it is not difficult to learn. Like the others, it is a 180° turn, 90° of which occurs on the push-off. All that the "flip" contributes is the other 90° without taking a breath, which does not call for the kind of gyrations that too many uninstructed or poorly-instructed learners go through.

Stroke Specifics

- The instructor needs to organize and plan for practice on both sides for the Crawl and Back Crawl.
- The instructor might first let Sidestroke swimmers glide into the wall on their favorite side and turn as with the other strokes. However, the swimmers will quickly complain that this turn brings them out on their non-favorite side. The instructor can then ask, "What does that tell you?" The obvious answer is that the swimmer who wishes to continue on the same side after the turn needs to reach for the wall with the **top** (non-leading) arm.
- For safety, teach the flip turn well away from the wall at first.

Self-Instruction

Self-instructed swimmers usually lack the desirable observation that an instructor with a trained eye provides. There may also be a shortage of discipline (in this case, self-discipline) that an instructor can provide. Additionally, the self-instructed too often have a tendency to feel guilty about not swimming laps. They will not temporarily sacrifice laps to practice the drills necessary to firmly establish each new stroke element to the point where the relearned skill can become automatic.

However, a trained instructor who has not read this book—even one who understands the Fundamentals and knows *what* corrections are needed—will be of little help without knowing *how* to produce such corrections for the swimmer. Thus, the self-instructed swimmer who has read this far may well be in a better position to become more efficient through self-instruction than under the guidance of an instructor who hasn't.

How can self-instruction be optimized? First, it is essential for you to concentrate on drills over laps. Increased stroke efficiency will produce more laps for the same time spent in the pool for years to come. Self-instruction does require self-discipline, patience, and faith in following the Rules.

Second, you need the motivation of seeing progress. The key to measuring the process of self-instruction, and what makes self-instruction acceptable to me, is your progress in developing more distance per stroke. Reducing the number of strokes per pool length is the best measure of stroke efficiency, and you don't need an instructor to count strokes.

Suppose you now take 30 strokes to swim a length, and through Rules One & Two, plus stroke drills, you are able to reduce that to 27 strokes. Even if you still swim at the same pace, you are reducing your time per length by 1/10, which is a 10% improvement in efficiency.

And when that efficient capability is extended beyond a single stroke and then beyond a single length, you will be able to swim more laps in a given workout period.

You can see by now that sacrificing the usual number of laps in order to drill for improved efficiency will be rewarded in the long term by longer, more comfortable swims.

Don't sell yourself short. Don't hurry. Have patience. Be sure to go back regularly to Getting Started and then to the Stroking page to remind yourself of the basics before you get focused on the mechanical details of individual strokes. Trust that your self-discipline and patience will be rewarded. And of course, be sure to enjoy the process as well as the results.

Appendix

Suggestions for Class Structure & Management

Here are a few general teaching suggestions to facilitate the learning process. Some may be old or obvious; others may merit your consideration or adoption.

Four Factors Relevant to Planning and Organizing a Class

1. **Location**—assumes a pool, regardless of size, especially since students will be taking only one or two good strokes at a time (Rule Two) to begin with. A lake bottom can be adapted, and often an instructor can make use of piers or deck supports to assist Getting Started.

2. **Timeframe**—whether it be a single lesson or a series of lessons (school quarter or semester). Between these two falls a clinic, consisting of one or a few 1- or 2-hour sessions, usually limited to a single stroke or two, related by transferable elements listed with each stroke in the Instructor section.

3. **Choice of stroke(s)**—or, with a series of lessons, a progression of strokes. Stroke order is covered in the Instructor section.

4. **The number of students**—while one-on-one teaching is the least complicated, an instructor need not be overwhelmed, even with up to thirty students or as many as can fit on one side of a pool. The instructor can have students perform all together or "do the wave" as individuals. But what works better is dividing a large class into two or three groups that proceed/perform sequentially. Consider using the wave formation

with six or more students, if only for variety. For a dozen or more, consider using a pair of groups or a trio.

Using groups keeps students from colliding and makes it easier to spot those who haven't followed the instructed movement. However, one has to avoid the boredom of grouping students by 1-2-3's every time or even using A-B-C's or X-Y-Z's. Use creativity for twos and threes, making them different (Rule One) every lesson. Think of local references or various duos or trios. Perhaps use "apples and oranges" for two groups, but add "kumquats" for the third. Try to use current pairs or trios (team names?), but using the names of the Three Stooges always seems to appeal to everyone.

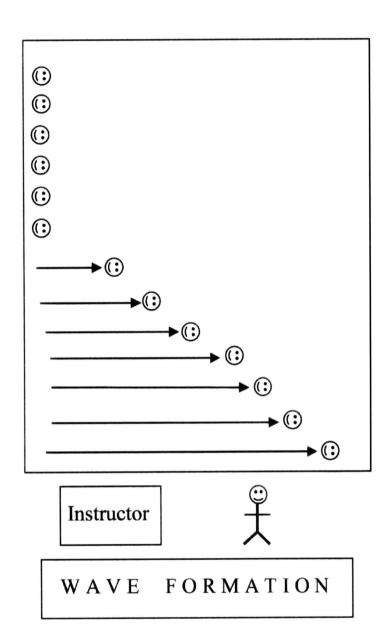

Instructor

WAVE FORMATION

173

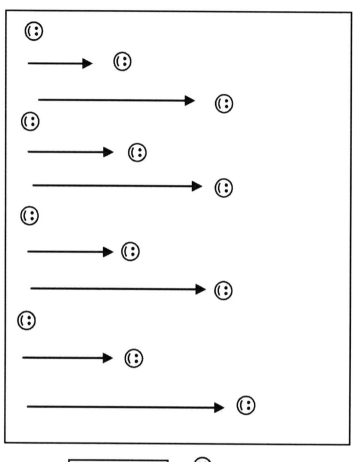

Instructor

GROUP FORMATION

Beyond the Four Factors

a) Adult swimmers are better able to understand kinesiological concepts basic to the efficiency of aquatic locomotion. However, instructors must be careful not to overwhelm students with knowledge of such concepts as Newton's Three Laws of Motion, Bernoulli's Principle, Froude's Law, long axis/short axis, lift versus drag, EVF, front quadrant, and other specifics best left unstated until or unless needed.

b) Keep talking to a minimum and students moving more. Use short phrases or single words as keys. Busy students have no time for reflection or negativity. However, explanation and amplification are possible for adult students, which is the distinguishing advantage they have over youngsters. Regardless, make a conscious effort to give individual attention to each student at least once during every class. This can be accomplished with a "Good, Joe" or "Nice stroke, Mary" or "Charlie, hold your glide a little longer before stroking."

c) An occasional demonstration is OK. If a picture is worth 1,000 words, using Jack Nelson's rope drill is worth 1,000 pictures (see section on Instructing for the Crawl Stroke). However, limit your demonstrations, remembering always that ultimately what counts is not what the instructor says or does, but what the student accomplishes. Be willing to do whatever works.

d) It is best not to use buoyancy aids, and not just because using aids causes dependency. For example, kickboards are wonderful for in-pool conversations, but they put the body on the stomach, both arms extended together, and the head out of water—none of which is an element of an efficient Crawl Stroke. The aids often end up floating or lying in various places around the pool, thus interfering with teaching efficiency instead of keeping the focus on instruction. And besides, students are not moving so far that they need aids.

e) Look to correct the disease and not the symptom. Consider the instructor who tells the Sidestroke student, "Your head comes up too high, and it bobs up and down." While this is true, the real problem is that the student's knees are separating vertically instead of horizontally. Fix the kick (disease) and you fix the head (symptom).

f) Follow Rule 1: use new skills or treat older skills in a way that the student has not encountered before. For instance, use exaggeration, such as ten kicks on each side before switching sides (see chapter on Crawl or Back Crawl). Another reason for exaggeration is that the learner is incapable of making small changes. For example, the swimmer whose Crawl Stroke entry crosses over beyond the long axis of the body, even if told or shown the proper entry for hand and arm, cannot make such a small modification. The swimmer needs to enter the hand at what feels like a 30° angle, perhaps even 45° or 60°. Occasionally, a 90° angle is needed ("feel like a crab or a spider") for the swimmer to get the feel of making the proper entry correction.

g) Follow Rule 2: There is nothing to be gained from performing or practicing inefficient movement. One implication of Rule 2 is a need for discipline, demanded by an instructor, or self-discipline developed by the swimmer, as well as for the patience to focus on quality over quantity. *Swim Better* requires a commitment to a series of successful steps to build a new and more efficient stroke. The value of long-term gains from the sacrifice of laps for drills should be the emphasis. This is addressed to a greater extent in the chapter on Self-Instruction.

h) Curiosity and creativity are greatly to be encouraged in the teaching process. Analogies always help. Cecil Colwin, one of the more creative swimming minds (see References section), uses "trap, wrap, unwrap" for phases in the Crawl Stroke. Terry Laughlin, founder of Total Immersion (TI), compares the rhythm of the Crawl and Back Crawl Strokes to ice skating, rollerblading, and cross-country skiing. His use of "grasping a ladder rung," where this author uses "over a barrel," may connect better with some swimmers. And the best teacher I know taught me "unpoint"—for toes—in recovering and then applying force for the whip kick.

i) Quality is always to be preferred over quantity.

Teaching Adult Beginners

Adult beginners are different from inefficient adult swimmers and, as such, need special instruction. However, the gap between the two can at times be quite narrow. Non-swimming beginners need just to get comfortable in the aquatic environment, and then they can Get Started the same from there. And from that point on, it is often easier for them to progress, not having anything to **un**learn.

Adults (again meaning teenagers and up) who have not yet begun to learn aquatic locomotion often may be embarrassed about it. They have had a long time to develop fears and defense mechanisms that require a different instructional approach. And, simply stated, fear is ignorance. It is the instructor's primary goal to overcome this built-up fear of the water.

Group learning is recommended. Psychology is vital. A group atmosphere provides unity for motivation, for support, and for mutual accomplishment. This is not to say that what works for a group cannot be modified for an individual. One-on-one teaching is not a separate problem. Personal lessons are the same as group lessons, though the length of any particular step varies for each student.

Otherwise, the strategies and tactics are pretty much the same as those used with previously weak swimmers: Keep students moving, with no time for reflection. Keep the instructional talk to a minimum. However, explanation is possible, depending on needs, which is what distinguishes adults from youngsters, who need little more than "Do this."

It is best to use no buoyancy aids, for several reasons. Kickboards and "pull-buoys," much less "eggs" or "swimmies" and the like, tend to place the beginner in an inefficient body position. Worse, they promote a false sense of security instead of a sense of self-reliance. Goggles are OK, and fins can be used later for drills.

But enough about theoretical concerns. Let's get on to the *how* of approaching adult beginners.

I love to sit down with a Beginning Swimming class of college students. Just by signing up for the course, they have indicated their underlying desire to succeed, even when they tell me, "No one has been able to get me to swim," or "I'm going to be a real challenge for you." Their idealistic goal is usually tempered by low expectations. Not that this is necessarily bad. To me, it just means that they will rejoice at the first signs of any unexpected progress.

As indicated above, psychology is vital, so I start by asking them why they aren't swimming already by this time in their lives. This encouragement becomes a sort of "True Confessions" session. At first, usually, students volunteer that they haven't had the opportunity. This may take a variety of forms and produce a few nodding agreements. Of course, I may challenge a senior by asking why that senior hasn't taken advantage of this present opportunity in the first three years. Then, sooner or later, the real reason comes out when someone volunteers—"I'm scared"—and is echoed by head nods or verbal confirmation throughout the group, most of whom have heretofore considered themselves alone in their fear.

My eventual response to them is to the effect that they are all in this together. No one is around to mock their efforts if and when they struggle. I tell them that fear is ignorance and that they can look forward to new knowledge as well as new skills. We will do only what we all can do before we attempt something new (Rule 2). That starts with asking who in the group would be banned from a Disney ride for being less than four feet tall. Of course, that means everyone can stand up in the pool and still stay alive, so that's where they all go.

Once in the shallow end of the pool, with a rope or other barrier clearly demarking the deep area, a few may cling to the wall for a moment or two, but all keep their balance and eventually move around against the water's resistance.

Now it's time for a game, whatever is available or works best. Basketball goals on the sides or a volleyball net setup are ideal, but the creative instructor will have prepared something equivalent. Make up sides and toss in an appropriate ball to get the game moving.

Pretty soon there is a focus on playing the game and less attention to the fact that it is being played in an aquatic environment. It makes for a fun first "lesson" that will motivate them to return for the next class. The game can also help to rid the class of possible "sandbaggers" who should not be there. Invariably, such a non-non-swimmer will subconsciously, in the heat of the game, take a stroke or few to get to the ball. I have made rare exceptions, but I like to rid the class of such "fakers," who could be a threat to class unity, as described above.

The next class requires them to earn their game for the day. They walk with knees bent and chins on the surface and/or whatever water adjustment skills are appropriate from texts or the instructor's creativity. This includes starting to open their eyes under water. I like to pair off beginners, each pair using two or three small but distinct metal objects (e.g., children's toy plane, train, car, or cars of different colors). One of the pair puts his face in the water to see and identify which of the toys is being held by the partner.

Without toys, or as a next step, one can see how many fingers the partner holds up under water. In doing so, they can be encouraged to go ever lower, facilitated by holding their breath or taking advantage of the law of physics that says, "Two things cannot occupy the same space at the same time." In other words, breathing out forcefully through the nose (mouth, too) prevents water from coming in. Let them experiment. Obviously, the partners take turns. The instructor's goal is to get everyone to about the same level of progress by the end of the teaching session and thus ready to go on together.

Once again, Rule Two is in effect. Until everyone succeeds, stop. Some may need a little extra individual attention, but use group motivation and keep the steps as small as necessary or as big as the group makes possible.

The next step is buoyancy. For this the instructor needs several sinkable objects. Diving rings are perfect, the metal toys may be used, but coins are usually too thin to pick up easily. As always, the reliance is on instructor creativity. Ben Franklin used a hard-boiled egg to do this, and thus this has become known as the Franklin Egg Trick. Again, pair off, this time for safety in case of lost balance.

Drop the object in, preferably, at least three feet of water. The students (one of each pair) stand, straight-legged and flat-footed, feet no more than shoulder-width apart, and attempt to pick up the object just in front of their feet without bending their knees. There may be an occasional heavily-muscled, non-buoyant athlete able to do this (Thurman Munson could walk across the pool under water.), but generally students will be frustrated at their lack of success.

After giving partners an equal opportunity to fail, the instructor can innocently ask what the problem is, and the students will say that their feet lift off the bottom when they try. The instructor can then ask, "What does this tell you?" The eventual conclusion they reach is that the normal tendency of the human body is not to sink, but to float. Literally and historically, Eureka!

The next step is for the students to take advantage of this new knowledge that decreases fear. They can hold their breaths, slide hands down their legs, grab their ankles, and maintain that floating position. Obviously, the progression is to letting go, into a comfortable jellyfish float, and they can see whether they can maintain this for ten, fifteen, or even thirty seconds. By now, they are not far from Getting Started.

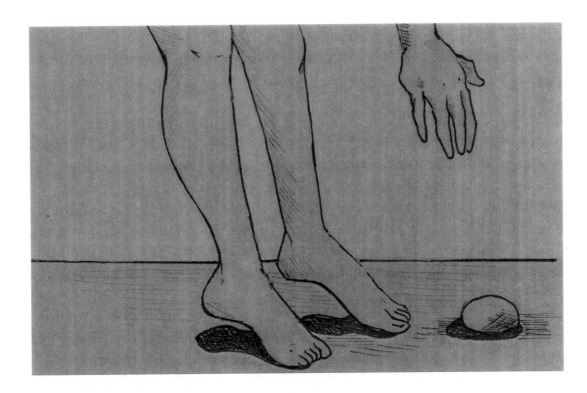

The beginners then progress to raising arms and legs, wide, from the jellyfish position toward a prone float, again helping each other make sure that everyone can safely reach this stage. Next, of course, is to start a prone float simply by extending arms on the surface and pushing feet off the bottom. Some may already have done so, with minimal horizontal motion to maintain buoyancy by counteracting gravity. The next step is to put arms together for a prone glide off the bottom. And that's really all it takes to be ready for Getting Started in shallow water.

There is no reason now to treat beginners differently from swimmers. Pushing off is far more essential to learning than floating. Now the beginner can generate momentum and minimize resistance. Even the rare non-floater is able to counteract gravity with propulsive horizontal force generated in Getting Started.

From this point, the beginner can progress to stroking in any order. However, I highly recommend that beginners first learn the Crawl Stroke, adding a comfortable kick on the side to maintain propulsion and an efficient body position, and then adding a single effective high-elbow arm stroke. Obviously, these are accomplished first on one side and then on the other. Don't forget Rule Two and unhurried progress. The focus is on one good stroke for everybody, eventually two, and always returning to the extended glide position on the side.

The Crawl Stroke chapter describes how to proceed from there to single-arm widths, the switch from side to side, adding breathing, etc. I like to use the rope drill (thumb pointing back is key) even for beginners to develop right away the Fundamental B feeling of anchoring the hand and moving the body past it (Page 151).

The recommended progression for beginners is then to the Back Crawl (consider it an inverted Crawl Stroke), and next to Elementary Back or Side or even to Butterfly. All these strokes transfer from the principles and positions already learned. Yes, there are beginners who can learn the Fly, simply as a double-arm Crawl Stroke.

Teaching the adult beginner can be challenging, but it can also be highly rewarding to realize that the beginner's **every** accomplishment is the result of your efforts. I wish you that satisfaction as your instructing career continues.

Scientific Support for Principles

Those who are interested in only the "how" of the various strokes and not the "why" miss a lot of the fun of coaching. It is the engagement of the intellect, as much as of the body, that makes swimming so challenging.
— Counsilman and Counsilman

The difficulty of changing highly learned, automatic skills is well documented. While my thoughts on this are speculative, I believe it is necessary to return a skill to deliberate levels under cognitive control in order to modify them. The challenge is then to return the modified skill to the automatic level of control.
— Prof. John Shea, Ph.D., specialist in Motor Learning, Indiana University, and veteran swim coach

The methodology behind Rules 1 & 2 was developed through experience, but it can be verified scientifically. Adult swimmers and their instructors share, as a common goal, the need to change the behavior associated with "swimming" or with "Crawl Stroke" or any other specific stroke. The learner has already-established psychomotor pathways; the behavior to be changed is both mental (cognitive) and physical. Surprisingly, according to several specialists in the field, there is next to nothing in the studies of Motor Learning regarding unlearning and relearning, so help for the swimmer and instructor comes primarily from the field of psychology, especially Learning Theory.

Adult swimmers have made inefficient swimming a habit. Edward Thorndike, an influential early 20th century psychologist, derived several Laws of Learning to explain behavior, including his Law of Repetition: "Other things being equal, exercise strengthens the bond between situation and response." The repetition of inefficient movement associated with "swimming" creates a formidable challenge to the instructor who wishes to rid the student of that association and then to restructure a more efficient habit of aquatic locomotion.

This implies that the student not be permitted any further repetition of inefficiency. As this book's Rule 2 implies, "If you are not behaving successfully (moving efficiently), stop." Richard Stiller, a more recent learning theorist, tells the instructor to interrupt the sequence of the habit, or change the setting in which it is usually triggered, in order to disrupt its patterns and pathways. Stiller cites William James, father of American psychology, to make his point: "Never allow an exception to occur until the new habit is thoroughly established."

Thorndike's Law of Association, that learning is facilitated by common elements from already-learned behavior, is here a threat to unlearning and thus is one of the bases of this book's Rule 1: "Make it different." The further the new behavior differs from the old, the better opportunity it has of replacing the old. It is very difficult to make subtle refinements. If behavior tends toward already established connections, then to change it requires that new connections be established that have minimal similarity to the old behavior. To repeat, the process of unlearning and relearning requires a deviation from an established mental/motor pattern or pathway and the acquisition of new associations.

So far, this has been a discussion of physical behavior only, the *visible* manifestation of what the instructor desires the student to learn or unlearn. Behaviorist psychology, exemplified by such notables as Thorndike and B. F. Skinner, considers only this directly-observable behavior and deems any intervening variables irrelevant.

By contrast, Gestalt psychology and field psychology consider also the nature of the learner, in particular the effect of the cognitive element on learning. E. C. Tolman's "purposive behaviorism" considers planning, inference, intention, and goal-oriented behavior. Like Tolman, educational psychologist Robert Gagné later says, "Learning is something that takes place inside an individual's head – in his brain." Habit restructuring is thus less neural than cognitive.

The cognitive aspect of behavior modification is involved in various aspects of learning:

Perception

It may not be necessary that a skill actually be different, only that it be perceived as such and thus not associated with past inefficiency. Whereas stimulus-response conditioning may explain animal behavior and learning, learning theorist Morris Bigge reminds us that "human beings do not simply respond to stimuli, they interpret them." Accordingly, learning is habit formation, and habits are goal-related. The basis of habit is in knowing what action will lead to what results. Intelligent behavior is thus purposive, learning being a process of searching out the conditions for the next step along the way.

Motivation

As a cognitive element, motivation is vital to the learning and relearning of physical skills. Attitudes such as awareness and readiness can either enhance or hinder the process. The instructor of adult swimmers has the advantage of students who are not children being forced to take swimming lessons. Just by opting for instruction, the adult swimmer is aware of inefficiency and is ready to do whatever will lead to greater efficiency.

Observation

Social-learning theorist Albert Bandura posits that learning "can occur on a vicarious basis by observing other people's behavior and its consequences for them."

A complex act (swimming) can be observed, but needs an instructor to pinpoint its essentials and break them down into sequential/progressive psychomotor elements. It is a "gradual shaping" process of deliberate steps.

Deliberate Movements

Repetition without meaning will not develop nor retain a new habit. During the learning process, the learner is vulnerable to a return to old habits, and distress precipitates relapse. Ideally, the swimmer should follow Rule 2 (master each step before adding another) and not be allowed to attempt stroking longer or harder than what the instructor dictates until the skill has become fully developed. However, the instructor usually has little control over the student's out-of-class behavior. Thus the instructor needs to emphasize the value of drills over yardage until the student is ready to handle full-stroke practice correctly.

The skill has to develop, as Dr. Shea notes at the head of this chapter, through cognitive control to the point where it becomes subconscious, from which time cognition can shift to focusing on a purposeful goal beyond mere efficient performance of the new skill.

My local instructing friend, Bob Hopkins, parallels Shea by positing a four-level sequence for reprogramming neuro-muscular memory: *unconscious incompetence*, *conscious incompetence*, *conscious competence*, and *unconscious competence*.

Reinforcement

Effective instruction requires feedback to enhance and retain desired behavior. Says Gagné, "Every act of learning requires feedback if it is to be completed." The anticipation of reinforcement, and the reinforcement itself—both cognitive elements—serve to motivate and to confirm desired behavior. For retention, Stiller says to reward new behavior, mostly by praise. Yet, food rewards, too, are possible for humans as well as for lab animals. I've seen some terrific swim-practice performances motivated by jelly beans or malted milk balls!

New behavior (i.e., correct repetition of swim stroke elements) is not reward enough. The instructor must give feedback to promote further correct performance—"Yes!" "Nice going!" "Way to go!" "Looks great!" Sometimes the feedback may be negative—"You've almost got it." "Don't stroke until your momentum slows down." "Keep your elbow higher than your hand"—but always with what the swimmer needs to fix in order to motivate and anticipate positive feedback. Of course, this can become more complicated within a group situation, where degree of success may vary, but the properly motivated group, realizing that their progress requires everyone to succeed, will motivate each other to help the whole group achieve success.

Transfer

Cognition plays a major role in the transfer of learning. Psycholgist Pedro Orata would go beyond Thorndike's Law of Association (transfer being facilitated by common elements) to say that transfer is "an attitude of response or a way of seeing the same kind of solution for different problems. Whereas senseless learning does not transfer, meaningful learning does." The instructor's job is not only to teach a physical skill, but also to be sure that the new skill is perceived and motivated properly.

The American Red Cross has advocated a phrase used frequently by contemporaries of Thorndike: Teach "from the Known to the Related Unknown." However, it is already understood here that there must be a *new* known to start the process. Because the *old* known is inefficient and needs to be unlearned, this book's Getting Started chapter begins the process that facilitates learning and solves new problems. The push-off and glide from the wall are essentially the same to begin all strokes and to complete all turns. This new behavior, therefore, must be perceived as such and motivated as essential to the student's overall goal of efficient aquatic locomotion.

Rules 1 and 2 establish a purposive framework for what the student is attempting to achieve—a cognitive as much as a strictly behavioral goal. Rule 1 leads to positive reinforcement for successful new stroking behavior that is different from what the student originally brought to the first class. Rule 2 could be considered negative reinforcement that prevents the recurrence of relapses into inefficient stroking. Together, the Rules combine to help adult students Swim Better and bring more lifelong enjoyment to swimmers willing to follow them.

Notes

References

References for Unlearning/Relearning

Bandura, Albert. "Social Learning Theory." In *International Encyclopedia of Psychiatry, Psychology, Psychoanalysis & Neurology,* vol. 10, edited by Benjamin B. Wolman. New York: Aesculopius, 1977.

Bigge, Morris L. *Learning Theories for Teachers,* 4th Edition. New York: Harper & Row, 1982.

Gagné, Robert M. *Essentials of Learning for Instruction.* Hinsdale, IL: Dryden Press, 1974.

Lawther, John D. *The Learning of Physical Skills.* Englewood Cliffs, NJ: Prentice-Hall, 1968.

Orata, Pedro T. "Recent Research Studies of Transfer of Training with Implications for the Curriculum, Guidance, and Personal Work." *Journal of Educational Research* 35 (October, 1941): 83.

Prochaska, James O., John C. Norcross, and Carlo C. DiClemente. *Changing For Good.* New York: William Morrow, 1994.

Skinner, B.F. *Science and Human Behavior.* New York: Macmillan, 1953.

Stiller, Richard. *Habits: How We Get Them, Why We Keep Them, How We Kick Them.* Valhalla, NY: Thomas Nelson, 1977.

Thorndike, Edward L. *Education.* New York: Macmillan, 1912.

Tolman, Edward C. *Purposive Behavior in Animals and Men.* New York: Century, 1932.

Annotated Swimming References and Recommended Reading

American Red Cross. *Swimming and Water Safety,* 3rd edition. Yardley, PA: StayWell, 2009. Great step forward for basic swim instruction.

Colwin, Cecil M. *Breakthrough Swimming.* Champaign, IL: Human Kinetics, 2002. For many years, our sport's foremost compiler.

Colyer, Robert J. "Feel for the Water: A Call for Research." *American Swimming* (July, 2009): 32-38.

Counsilman, James E. *The Science of Swimming*. Englewood Cliffs, NJ: Prentice-Hall, 1968. Simply the bible of our sport.

Counsilman, James E. *The Application of Bernoulli's Principle to Human Propulsion in Water*. Bloomington: Indiana University Publications, 1971. Short brochure, first confirmation of Fundamental B.

Counsilman, James E. and Brian E Counsilman. *The New Science of Swimming*. Englewood Cliffs, NJ: Prentice-Hall, 1994. Update of First Edition with later research and practices.

Drollette, D. "Swim like a Fish," *New Scientist 2145* (August 1, 1998): 36-39. World champions coached by slow and precise stroking.

Hines, Emmitt. *Fitness Swimming*, 2nd edition. Champaign, IL: Human Kinetics, 2008. *Swim Better* approach to competitive adult Masters swimmers.

Laughlin, Terry. *Extraordinary Swimming for Every Body*. New Paltz, NY: Total Immersion, 2006. *Swim Better* from a different and more extensive approach.

Laughlin, Terry. *Total Immersion*, revised & updated edition. New York: Simon and Schuster, 2004. Successful system based on principles behind *Swim Better*.

Maglischo, Ernest W. *Swimming Faster*. Palo Alto, CA: Mayfield Publishing, 1992. Showed him as worthy successor to Counsilman.

Maglischo, Ernest W. *Swimming Fastest*. Champaign, IL: Human Kinetics, 2003. Literally and figuratively, our sport's *magnum opus*.

Silvia, Charles E. *Manual and Lesson Plans for Basic Swimming, Life Saving, Water Stunts, Springboard Diving, Skin and Scuba Diving, and Methods of Teaching*. Springfield, MA: The Author, 1970. Still the best description of how hands and feet function for swimming.

Acknowledgments

While this book's approach to teaching swimming may be unique, it originates from a lifetime of experience and the influence of so many of my fellow instructors and coaches, from their writings and my on-deck observations. Those who have read my drafts have had a positive effect on the final work.

Appreciation goes to aquatic professional Terri Lees and to my classmate Bob Irvine for their textual suggestions, and especially to editor Alex Eguiguren, who somehow was able to visualize this intended outcome from the fragmented elements of those early drafts.

The illustrations would not have been possible without the combined efforts of Benita and Georg Koman, who graciously provided the use of their pool; and Rob and Denise Schindler and their daughter Sarah, who volunteered as our swimmer/model.

About the Author

Bob Colyer is a Dartmouth College graduate (magna cum laude, Phi Beta Kappa) with a Master of Arts in Teaching English from Wesleyan University. After years as a club and high school coach, he earned his doctorate under the legendary James "Doc" Counsilman at Indiana University. His successful college teaching and coaching career, including ten years as NCAA Swimming Records Chair, earned him the Master Coach award from the College Swim Coaches Association of America. He has been a swim official on all levels and in retirement continues to conduct stroke clinics. His monograph on "Feel for the Water: A Call for Research" was published in *American Swimming* magazine (2009, Issue 2). His "Thoughts on Breathing" appeared in the same publication in 2013. He can be reached at bobcolyer@yahoo.com.

Notes

Notes

Notes

CPSIA information can be obtained at www.ICGtesting.com
Printed in the USA
LVOW10s1818120215

426759LV00011B/372/P